Awakening

Awakening

A Daily Guide to Conscious Living

Shakti Gawain

NEW WORLD LIBRARY · SAN RAFAEL · CALIFORNIA

© 1991 Shakti Gawain
Published by New World Library
58 Paul Drive, San Rafael, CA 94903

Front cover photo and interior photos:
Dean Campbell
Back cover photo: Susan Schelling
Cover design: Kathleen Vande Kieft
Text design: Abigail Johnston
Typography: Harrington-Young, Albany, California
Indexing: AMC Indexing

First printing, September, 1991
Printed in the U.S.A. on acid-free paper
10 9 8 7 6 5 4 3 2 1
ISBN 0-931432-86-3

ACKNOWLEDGMENTS

I would like to acknowledge my editor, Leslie Keenan, for her creative ideas, support, and hard work in putting this book together. Thanks to my husband, Jim Burns, for the many levels of support which made it possible to get this book done. And thanks to all the dedicated people at New World Library who make these books and tapes possible.

DEDICATION

For Manuela,
with love and appreciation.

Many of us in the world today are on a consciousness journey. We are seeking to bring our individual
and collective lives into greater alignment with
natural laws and universal principles, so that we
can live in balance and harmony with ourselves,
one another, and the earth. Today, with the ecologi-
cal, social, and political challenges we face in addi-
tion to our personal issues, it is essential that we
learn to live more consciously. By individually taking responsibility to live our lives with awareness,
we can set examples that will empower others in
our world to do the same.

Learning to live our daily lives with consciousness is an ongoing, ever-deepening, lifetime process. It requires that we contact our essential
spiritual wisdom and integrate it into all other
levels of our being—mental, emotional, and physical. It challenges us to recognize and release old
patterns and beliefs and to open to new ways in
every area of our lives.

I hope this book may be a help to you in your
daily life. Each daily entry has a heading, a short
message, and an affirmation or question. You may

**
**

Winter

**
*

Awakening

Each morning as we awaken we have the opportunity to begin our lives anew, with a fresh perspective gained from what we learned the day before and the refreshment from our night's rest.

The beginning of each new year represents a special opportunity to awaken to a new level of consciousness, with all the wisdom we have gained from the previous year's experiences. Day by day and year by year we proceed on our journey of awakening into consciousness.

*

Each day,
and each year,
I am awakening to greater
consciousness.

*

The journey of consciousness

Becoming conscious means becoming increasingly aware of what's going on inside us and around us. We've all lived in a certain level of denial, and we are in the process of awakening from that unconsciousness. Consciousness is not about fixing ourselves or improving ourselves. It's about coming to know ourselves in all our many aspects and thereby living life more fully. The journey of consciousness is lifelong. But, when you really think about it, what else is there to do?

*

I *am*
on a lifelong journey of
conscious awakening.

*

Honor yourself

You are unique. You are a valid and special part of the universe. You are important. You are here to create in your own very special way, a way no one else can. Know this, in the deepest core of your being.

*

I am unique.
I am contributing to
the universe in my own special way,
right now.

*

What do you want?

We all want certain things, although we may not always be conscious of what they are. If we can get in touch with what we want, we can create it. Because simply by becoming conscious of our desires, we begin to manifest them in our lives.

*

*I am becoming
conscious of my deepest needs
and desires.*

*

Set goals

Once you are conscious of what you want, you can begin to take the next step, which is setting goals. To receive what you desire, you must take some action toward it. This action is not complicated. Simply write down what your goals are for the coming year, for the next five years. Writing them doesn't mean you have to stick to them. Your goals are always evolving and changing. But you must recognize and acknowledge what they are now. Then you can begin to move forward.

*

*What are
my goals for this year?
For the next five years?*

*

We get what we desire

The universe is designed to give us everything we need and want. It's really our own fears and our feelings of unworthiness, shame, and doubt that keep us from receiving the incredible abundance and fullness and goodness of life.

*

*As I learn
to trust in the universe,
I am receiving everything
that I desire.*

*

We create our own reality

We create our own reality every moment, whether or not we're conscious of it. If we're not conscious, we create it out of habit and old patterns. As we become more and more conscious, we are more able to create what we truly desire.

*

I *am*
creating my own reality,
every day.

*

Our lives are our creation

We need to acknowledge how incredible our lives already are and therefore how powerful we are. We have all created a great many unique, interesting, even amazing experiences in our lives so far. We have attracted a number of fascinating characters into the drama of our personal reality. These people and experiences are all mirrors of our creativity. Although we are all capable of creating even better and more satisfying realities, what we have already manifested is strong proof of how powerful our beings really are.

*

*My life
is an expression of my own
creativity.*

*

Life is simple

Life is much simpler than most of us think it is. We struggle so hard, trying to improve ourselves, trying to grow, trying to become conscious, trying to achieve in the world. We need to relax, open up, and allow ourselves to receive from the life force within us and all around us. Life is always trying to bring us everything we want and need, but most of the time we're moving so fast and trying so hard that we don't notice!

*

I am open
to receiving whatever comes my way
today.

*

We each have a direct line to the truth

We each have the wisdom of life within us, and we each have a direct line to that truth at every moment. If we can listen to and trust our intuition, it will guide us. It will show us step by step what we need to do and what we need to know, every moment of our lives, if we let it.

*

My intuition
is guiding me
through life.

*

Life is an exploration

Life is an exploration. We need to liberate ourselves to think of it that way. We tend to take everything we do too seriously and feel that every action must produce the desired results. When we can instead think of life as an exploration, we're free to try more things. We can *explore* our options, *discovering* many different aspects of ourselves in the process. This attitude creates more possibilities for us.

If some of the things you try don't work, just let them go. Don't think that if you start something you must finish it. It's okay to explore and learn from that process of discovery.

*

I am
willing to explore something
new.

*

Live with passion

What do you do out of guilt or because you think you should? Ask yourself instead what it is that you truly *desire* to do. Do what feels right, and that will bring you satisfaction. Live your life with passion, in a way that is meaningful and fun.

How can we create a world of fulfillment and joy unless we begin to live so in each moment?

*

As I *let go*
of ''shoulds'' and the feeling of guilt,
I *do what brings me*
joy.

*

Spontaneity

Spontaneity is the quality of living in the moment and truly following our own energies, moving fully and freely with the life force. It's a wonderful feeling to allow ourselves to be totally spontaneous.

Our culture generally values structure, planning, and discipline over spontaneity. Spontaneity is equated with childhood. Even as children, many of us were forced to control our spontaneity. Certainly as adults we are expected to behave in a rational, contained manner. So most of us have lost our connection with our true spontaneous spirit. One of the most profound things you can do in your healing process is to reconnect with your natural spontaneity.

*

Each day,
I am learning to move more fully and freely
with the life force.

*

Loss of spontaneity contributes
to addiction

One way some people deal with the suppression of their natural spontaneous spirits is by using drugs. Alcohol and certain other drugs temporarily paralyze the "censoring" part of the psyche that tends to repress anything that may not be socially acceptable. This allows for a temporary outburst of spontaneous energy. Unfortunately, this outburst takes place in a distorted, unnatural, and destructive way and ultimately leads to further suppression.

The healing process requires that we give up manipulating ourselves with artificial substances and get to know our own psyches. We must find the support we need to learn to trust our natural, feeling selves and to allow them to express in healthy ways in our lives.

*

I express myself
spontaneously in natural, creative,
healthy ways.

*

Spontaneity can feel like
losing control

Spontaneity can feel frightening because it means giving over our own preplanned ideas and trusting in the moment, letting the spirit flow through us. It means taking a risk and letting go of control. It's hard at first, particularly if we've been taught not to trust spontaneity. But when we feel that connection to the moment, it's very fulfilling. When we are free to follow our own spontaneous feelings, we are open to the universe and we allow for more opportunities and more creativity in our lives.

Start with allowing yourself to be more spontaneous in small ways, at times when you feel relatively safe. Spontaneity will grow naturally, as you learn to trust it.

*

I am trusting
the universe and allowing it to work
through me.

*

Discipline can support fun

Some people are very spontaneous. They respond to life in a very emotional way and are often oriented toward pursuing pleasure and fun. They are usually creative, artistic, and fascinating to be around. Sometimes they suffer from lack of success or recognition in the world because they fear and lack the quality of discipline and structure. They need to learn that discipline can support fun, and it can support creativity. It can support enjoyment in life. It doesn't have to mean stifling their spirit; it's just bringing their lives into balance.

*

I *am*
learning to balance discipline
and spontaneity.

*

The balance between spontaneity
and discipline

Spontaneity and discipline work together in your life. It's good to have structure and organization when you are trying something new to help you feel safe and to give you direction. Discipline supports the process of learning. It gives you some sense of what you're doing and some confidence. Then, as you master the technical aspects, you can be more spontaneous.

Discipline can give us certain technical tools and a certain kind of structure that then supports the creative spirit. When you are learning to play music, you must play scales at first. Then, as you master the scales, you become spontaneous in expressing your own feeling and improvising, allowing the spirit to flow through you.

*

Through discipline
and spontaneity, I express myself
creatively.

*

*Create positive structure
in your life*

Whether you need more spontaneity or more discipline, setting up a structure in your life can help support you in finding a balance of those qualities. Each of us needs to work a certain number of hours per day, play a certain amount of time each day, and have some time each day for relaxation. We need time to accomplish our tasks and time for intimacy with loved ones. Most of us have some difficulty establishing the right balance. We need to create a daily and weekly schedule that allows time for all our basic needs to be met.

*

I am
*creating a balanced schedule
for myself.*

*

Find your own rhythm

It's very important to create a schedule that really gives you what you want, so you won't be tempted to rebel against it. If your schedule includes only what you should be doing and doesn't allow you the time for what you want to be doing, then it won't work; you'll throw it out. Also, build into your structure open times and space for spontaneity. You are trying to give yourself room for creativity, not stifling it.

Make a list of your priorities, and the amount of time each takes. Take into account your responsibilities and the needs of people around you. Then put them into a weekly schedule. Find your own rhythm. Do what pleases you, what works for you, what makes you feel balanced and adds to your sense of well-being.

*

I am finding
a balance in my life of work and play,
of my responsibilities to others
and to myself.

*

Perfection is in process

Human life by its very nature is filled with vulnerabilities, trial and error, and learning. Expecting
ourselves to behave in some perfect way or to attain
perfect results is not realistic.

We need to shift the focus from trying to attain
perfect results or to live up to perfect standards to
recognizing the innate perfection in the process or
in the journey. The life force has an incredible
perfection about it. As we're learning to recognize
and follow the life force, we will see the perfection of
the process, how everything we need to learn is
brought to us in some amazing way that we could
never have figured out or understood.

*

*I accept
the perfection of
my process.*

*

Trust your higher power

There is some higher intelligence at work in us. It knows what it's doing and is trying moment by moment to guide us, show us, teach us, and love us. It is trying to help us become all that we can be. In order to do that, it has to guide us through our own healing process. At times this may be uncomfortable. But eventually we are able to see the necessity and perfection of each step we have taken on the journey.

*

I am learning
to recognize and accept my higher power.
I am learning to trust and
rely on it.

*

We are already where
we need to be

As human beings we are always trying to get somewhere. Many of us seek some standard of success that we think will bring happiness or validation from the world. Even those of us involved in the personal growth and consciousness process still have the idea that we certainly don't want to be where we are—we're trying to get somewhere better. And when we get to that place, everything will be right somehow. Yet, consciousness cannot be found somewhere else; it happens through becoming aware of where we are right now.

Trying to get somewhere else takes us away from appreciating the process. When we begin to enjoy the process itself, we can stop worrying and become completely involved in the fascinating journey that's unfolding each moment in each day.

*

Today I am not trying
to get somewhere else. I'm focusing on being aware of
where I am now.

*

We are students

We all have a tendency to criticize ourselves. We're very good at figuring out what's wrong or inadequate about ourselves. We're constantly beating ourselves because we don't do everything exactly right and because we aren't already perfect. It hurts to live that way. If you're beating yourself up, you can't learn. We're here to learn. We're in school. We're children. If we were already enlightened, we wouldn't be here.

*

Life
is my school, and I'm here
to learn.

*

*You have a teacher
within you*

You have a teacher within you. It's your own higher self. It's always with you every moment, whether you feel it or not. All we ever need to do is go inside ourselves and ask for guidance, ask for truth, ask for the support, love, or encouragement we need. When we ask for guidance, it begins to come to us right away. It doesn't always come in the way that we think it should, but it always comes.

*

*My intuitive wisdom
is guiding me step by step along
my own special path.*

*

Messages are all around us

Messages from the universe come through in extraordinary ways. Very literal and very specific things can happen to show you what your own soul is trying to communicate to you. You may have to let go of some rational conditioning even to entertain the idea that there could be a higher force that knows what it's doing and is trying to communicate with you. But if you do open up to the idea that a higher power is trying to guide you, you will start to get messages from your intuition, from your dreams, from simply watching the events of your life.

*

I am
becoming aware of all the messages
from the universe.

*

Life is never trying to tell us
there's something wrong with us

The universe is always trying to show us how we can be more of who we are. The painful lessons that we get inevitably show us that we are not trusting or loving ourselves, or that we are not expressing ourselves honestly or taking care of ourselves properly. In some way, we are not fully honoring our relationship with ourselves. The universe is trying to show us how we can express our power, truth, and creativity in our lives, and how we can love and trust ourselves more.

*

I honor myself
for who I am. Each day I am becoming
more and more myself.

*

Embrace the hard times, too

Accept what comes to you today. There is great richness, even in the times that are uncomfortable. Of course, we wish we could get through those times faster, but each time we move through something that's painful, or confusing, or dark, or difficult in some way, it makes it a little easier to trust that there will be a positive result.

When you become fascinated with the process itself, you can use everything as a learning experience. It doesn't take as long before you can look at the situation and see what it's about, or see why you need to go through it, or see what you are getting out of it.

*

*I embrace
my experience now as part of my
learning process.*

*

Every day is filled with gifts

Every day is filled with many lessons and teachings, which are really gifts in disguise. Often, we resist these experiences at first, wishing something else were happening instead! The learning process is easier if we can learn to say to ourselves, "Life is giving me a gift right now. It's teaching me something about myself, something that I really want to learn. Look how much I've learned already. Look at how far I've come. Now here's the next thing that I need to learn." Sometimes these experiences feel painful, but when we receive the healing in them, we can recognize and feel thankful for the gifts they bring.

*

What gifts
am I receiving from the universe today?
What do I need to learn?

*

Look for the humor in life

The universe has a good sense of humor, if you're willing to observe it. As you begin to see your life as a journey that's unfolding in some kind of order with a specific purpose, you start to see the hand of the universe in all kinds of humorous, playful, and even mischievous ways. Coincidences or synchronicities occur, or ironic things happen if you are open to seeing them.

*

As I
open to the playfulness in
the universe, I see its humor
in many ways.

*

Ask your higher power

When you're feeling confused or uncertain, when you don't know what direction to go, or what you need or what you're supposed to be learning, just ask. It's hard to remember to do this, but it's very important. On a daily basis, ask what direction you should go or what you need to know or what you are learning from this experience. Keep asking, and stay open until the answers come. If you're still not sure, you can ask for a sign. Stay open to whatever comes.

*

When I ask
my higher power, the answer is
revealed to me.

*

Love yourself

Love yourself for having the courage to come to the physical plane and for attempting this very difficult journey. Love yourself for the connection that you have to the power of the universe. Love yourself for your wonderful humanness, your vulnerability, your confusion, even your ignorance. Love yourself for the child that you are. You are here in your innocence to grow and to learn.

*

I
love and respect
myself.

*

Fear of emptiness

To the degree that we've disconnected from the essence of our spirit and the life force of the universe, we feel an emptiness inside us, a loneliness, a sense of lack. This is terribly frightening, so we create activities to keep us busy and thus avoid those feelings. If we stopped all the frenetic activity, we would feel our essential emptiness and meaninglessness. Of course, that's exactly what we have to do. Ironically and paradoxically, when we move into the emptiness, we open to being able to reconnect with spirit and be filled again from our spiritual source.

*

I *am*
connecting with my deep,
inner feelings.

*

Stillness

Stillness is something our culture doesn't value and is somewhat afraid of. We don't cultivate the art of stillness, which is essentially meditation— stilling the physical, emotional, and mental levels enough to experience the spiritual level. In stillness we stop the frenetic activity and confront that inner place of emptiness or loneliness. By staying with the painful feelings long enough to move through them, we contact our deepest essential selves and reconnect with a universal sense of oneness with all.

Stillness can be a very blissful state, if you allow yourself to be physically, mentally, and emotionally still long enough to really connect with spirit.

*

I *am*
cultivating the art of
stillness.

*

Take time for stillness each day

It's crucial to find time for a little quiet moment with yourself each day. The two easiest times for most people to find some stillness or to do some meditation are fairly early in the morning, before getting completely caught in the day's activities, or in the evening, after the day's main events are complete.

Finding stillness can be extremely powerful, even if it's just for a very short time. Don't think that you have to meditate for an hour or even half an hour. Five or ten minutes can be very helpful if you know how to relax and drop into the deepest place you can find in that short a time. Drop out of your mind, down into your being. It feels like falling with a very soothing feeling into a certain place. If your mind is too active and there's too much going on, you may not fall into that place. Through practice, you can learn to drop in fairly quickly.

*

Today, and every day,
I take time to find
stillness.

*

Becoming whole

The universe consists of an infinite number of essential qualities, energies, or archetypes. All these energies exist within each of us. Our task in becoming whole, realized human beings is to develop and express as many as possible of these qualities in our lives, as fully as we can. Life is always guiding us in the direction that will help us develop the qualities we most need.

*

Every experience
along my journey is helping me
become whole.

*

Paradox

The nature of the physical plane is duality. That means that for every truth there's an equal and opposite truth. This seems paradoxical to us and is difficult for us to accept because we have such a habit of linear thought. For the logical, left-brained side of us, this paradox is difficult to comprehend. We need to draw from our more intuitive, right-brained, holistic selves to understand the whole and to see that truth comes in pairs of opposites. We need to explore and understand all those opposites.

*

I accept
the paradoxes in my life
and open to learning
from them.

*

Life is filled with polarities

Life is filled with opposites and polarities. When we can actually contain and include and embrace all those opposites of life within ourselves, when we actually have the capacity to express all those opposites, then we're full, conscious, enlightened human beings. And until we have all those opposites we aren't yet complete.

*

All the polarities
of life exist within
me.

*

*The way to one quality
is through its opposite*

In order to fully express one energy it is necessary to integrate its opposite polarity. It can even be said that the way to one quality is through its opposite. For example, you can be truly strong only to the degree that you've accepted and embraced your weakness or vulnerability. In order to be a great teacher you must also be willing to learn. And one who is truly wise is one who accepts one's own foolishness.

*

*I am opening
to experiencing new energies,
opposite from those most
comfortable to me.*

*

Life guides us toward
our opposite

Most of us are very good at accepting and expressing one side of a polarity and not so good at
accepting and expressing the other side of it. Or, we
may stay in the safe middle ground, but be afraid to
express either extreme. If we're identified with one
polarity, life always pushes us toward its opposite. If
we're comfortable in the middle, it may push us in
both directions or it will guide us in one direction
and then in another. In many cases, it does this
through our relationships. The people we are in
relationship with tend to push us toward expressing the part of ourselves we haven't yet learned
to express.

*

What qualities
do I feel comfortable with
and know how to express? What are some
opposite qualities to these? How comfortable
do I feel with them?

*

Contain the opposites

Dealing with polarities means not rejecting the parts of ourselves that we're not comfortable with. It means expanding to include them. Think of yourself as a circle, with your various polarities at opposite ends. Instead of pulling away from some parts, make the circle bigger.

*

*I am expanding
to embrace the polarities
in my life.*

*

No part of us is negative

We judge some of our feelings, thoughts, and energies as negative, and we classify other aspects of ourselves and of life as positive. We attempt to get rid of the negative things and experience only the positive things. But the things we call negative are just the things we're afraid of or don't understand. We don't want to experience them so we call them negative. We make them bad and try to get rid of them. But they can never go away, because they are a part of us and a part of life.

*

*I am willing
to look at the "negative" sides
of my self.*

*

What part of yourself
are you blocking?

By blocking the energy we have stored in our "negative" sides, and by using more energy to keep it blocked, we are limiting our own power. By spending more and more of our energy trying to keep the door shut on the closet of our "negative" selves, trying not to experience aspects of ourselves that we think are negative and frightening, we drain our life force. We actually die from using our energy to close off our energy!

Life is trying to teach us how to open the door and begin to look at those parts of ourselves that we've been frightened of, that we've hated, that we think are bad and ugly and awful and scary. Life is helping us to discover the hidden aspects of ourselves that we need, that we want, that we can't really live without.

*

I am
learning to accept all sides
of myself.

*

Everything in the universe
wants to be loved

Whatever you don't like, whatever you reject, whatever you try to get away from or get rid of, sticks to you. It bugs you and pursues you. It flies right in your face. The reason is because everything in the universe wants to be loved. It's such a simple principle!

All creation wants to be loved and appreciated and included in life. Any quality or energy you are not experiencing or expressing in your life comes after you until you accept it and integrate it.

*

Is there someone or something
that has been bothering me?
Could it represent some part of myself
that wants to be loved?

*

You are a multifaceted being

It's essential for us to accept that we have many conflicting aspects to our personalities. We can't expect ourselves to be totally consistent. Instead, we have to take a perspective of embracing all the conflicting and varied aspects of ourselves and seeing ourselves as multifaceted beings. How can we expand enough to allow all our many facets to shine and express themselves in our lives?

*

*I rejoice in
and express all the facets of
my being.*

*

The love affair of the universe

The two essential principles of life are expressed in eastern philosophy as yin and yang—male and female. The pulsation of energy between these two polarities creates the dance of life.

The feminine principle within us is the receptive, intuitive, feeling aspect of ourselves. The masculine principle expresses itself in our strength and ability to focus and take action. As we bring these two aspects of ourselves into balance, harmony, and union, we create the love affair of the universe within our own being.

*

The love affair
of the universe is expressing itself
in my life.

*

The polarities within us

Here are a few sets of opposite qualities or polarities:

Masculine	Feminine
Doing	Being
Active	Passive
Rational	Intuitive
Strong	Vulnerable
Organized	Spontaneous
Material	Spiritual
Serious	Playful
Responsible	Carefree
Giving	Receiving
Intellectual	Emotional

Which ones do you feel comfortable with and / or express in your personality? Which ones do you need to accept or develop?

*

*I am learning
to accept and develop my opposite
polarities.*

*

We need to balance
being and doing

Two of the most basic and important polarities we need to balance are the energies of being and doing. Being is the ability to be fully present in the moment with an open, receptive awareness— simply experiencing. Doing is the ability to move through time with focused attention to accomplish a specific task.

Being is the essence of feminine energy. Doing is the essence of masculine energy. As a man or a woman, we each have both these energies. Most of us are more comfortable with one of these polarities than the other, and therefore we've developed one ability more than the other. To live balanced lives, however, we need to fully develop our capacity for both being and doing.

*

Today
I am taking time for being
and doing.

*

*Appreciate the value
of being*

In our culture, male energy is more respected and understood than is female energy. Therefore, doing is more highly valued and cultivated than being. In fact, being is not seen as a legitimate or important way to spend time. If we are not actively doing or accomplishing something, we feel we are "wasting time." Because of this cultural bias, most of us push ourselves to do more than our natural energy would allow. We constantly deplete and exhaust ourselves, using caffeine and other stimulants to keep ourselves going. Even men and women who are good at being and spend more of their time that way often do not respect themselves or receive respect from others for their ability to be. We need to value being.

*

I

*value time spent in
being.*

*

Cultivate the art of being

It's time to cultivate and appreciate the art of being. Being is a deeply fulfilling and satisfying experience that allows us to commune with our deeper spiritual selves, with nature, and with each other. Time spent in being replenishes and renews our energy; heals our bodies, minds, and spirits; fills us with inspiration; and makes life worth living.

*

*I am
learning the art of
being.*

*

Being is unfamiliar

Being is so unfamiliar to many of us that it can be scary. We're addicted to doing in our society. We're programmed that we have to be doing something all the time and that if we are not producing something, we are wasting our time. We may try to give ourselves being time, but become impatient and think that nothing worthwhile is happening. Yet, being time is very important. Not only does it nourish us and replenish our energies so that we can continue to give and do, but it's also a time to connect with our inner guidance and inspiration.

*

Today and every day
I give myself time just to be,
without doing anything.

*

Two ways of getting what you want

The masculine and feminine energies within us have two different modes for creating what they want in life. The male energy gets what it wants through doing—going after it and making it happen. The feminine energy gets what it wants through being—by magnetizing and opening to receive what it desires. We need to develop both principles. We need to go after it and make it happen when that's called for, and we need to relax and allow it to come to us when that's appropriate.

*

I *am*
developing both my masculine and feminine
modes of creating what I want
in my life.

*

Discover your primary mode

When it comes to getting our needs met in life, most of us have relied more on one mode of operating than the other. Either we're comfortable with an active, masculine style of pursuing our goals and distrust the more receptive ways of being, or we rely on our female energy to attract what we want and feel uncomfortable with the more direct male approach. Either way, we need to appreciate our primary mode and focus on developing its opposite.

*

What is my primary mode
of getting what
I want?

*

Develop your opposite mode

If you are good at going after what you want, you may need to develop your ability to relax and draw things and people to you. If you tend to hold back and wait for things to come to you, you may need to risk pursuing your goals more actively. Stretch to explore another side of yourself.

Pick the affirmation that helps you develop your less-familiar mode, or use both:

*

I am
learning to get what I want through:
a. direct, focused, assertive action
b. relaxed, receptive being

*

Too many options

In this day and age, a very real problem is having too many options. It can be difficult to make the choices necessary to simplify our lives because there's a tremendous fear that if we say no to anything, we'll miss out. We want to go everywhere and do everything. This is an overactive expression of our male energy. The male energy in us seeks satisfaction through external exploration and discovery. This energy is wonderful, unless it's out of balance.

*

I *am*
letting go of unnecessary
options.

*

Finding simplicity

To find balance, we need to move inside and connect to our female energy. The feminine energy has a sense of fulfillment and contentment in the moment, from within. It connects us with our inner source. From there we can ask, "What do I truly want and need? What direction do I really need to go?" We can determine what activity is necessary and meaningful, and let the rest go. Life can become simpler and more fulfilling.

*

What are my most important
priorities today? Can I let go of some things
that are not as important?

*

Life need not be a struggle

We've inherited a deep core belief system from our parents and our culture that life is a struggle and that we must make a great deal of effort to get our needs met and achieve our goals. But it doesn't have to be that way. This concept is very difficult for many of us to accept because anything other than struggle feels strange and unfamiliar. We can begin to release the struggle and allow life to become easier. Of course there are challenges and times of difficulty in every life. But essentially, life is meant to follow a simple, natural flow.

*

Today I am
releasing my need to struggle.
I am allowing my life to become easier
now.

*

We are addicted to struggle

Struggle is very familiar. In a way, it's comfortable. We're good at struggling. Confronting challenges, working on goals—these are easy. But when we begin to get the things that we've always wanted in life, it can be disconcerting. A part of us will say, "Wait a minute, where's the struggle? Is this okay? Is it okay for things to be easy?" It can be frightening or confusing. We are used to filling our lives with effort, and when things start to get easier, the open space may feel uncomfortable. Having things come to us and receiving what we've always wanted can be a challenge!

*

It's okay
for my life to be
easy.

*

Sickness can be a signal
that you need being time

If you don't give yourself the relaxation time you need, your body may have to make it happen. The body will create an emotional breakdown, or become physically sick, or just feel tired and lacking in energy. People who need being or quiet time and don't allow it or don't know how to give it to themselves may find their bodies will refuse to function.

Usually bodies get sick when we need time to slow down, time to be quiet, time to go inside, time to go through some internal change, or time just to recuperate from the amount of energy we put out.

*

I *am*
paying attention to what my body tells me.
I *give myself the rest*
I *need.*

*

Boredom

Boredom is one thing we experience when our life force is blocked in some way. Usually it's because there's an emotion or feeling we're afraid to experience and so we go into boredom instead. Underneath it there's sadness, grief, anger, or fear that we don't want to feel. So we stop ourselves from feeling. Anytime we stop ourselves from feeling, we stop the life force, and an experience of boredom can be the result.

Life is never boring. If we're experiencing boredom it's because we're stuck—our energy is stuck or blocked in some way. We need to look into that feeling and ask, "Where am I stuck? How and why am I blocking myself? What feeling is underneath this?"

*

Whenever I
experience boredom, I look inside
to discover what my real feelings
are.

*

Waste time

For many of us "wasting" time is the ultimate sin! If this is true for you, it can be very consciousness expanding to make yourself spend some time each week in completely meaningless activity. Choose something that is pleasurable, but has no other redeeming value—read a trashy magazine, play a game, lie in bed, or whatever. Enjoy yourself and don't feel guilty. You deserve it.

*

Once in a while,
I waste time in a frivolous
diversion.

*

Let your feelings flow

Very few of us understand how to handle our emotions in a natural, healthy way. We live in a culture that is terrified of feeling too much. We have all learned many ways to deny, repress, manipulate, or try to change our emotions. We get stuck holding onto certain emotional patterns because they feel familiar and safe. What we don't know how to do is simply accept and respect our feelings and allow them to flow through us in their own natural rhythms.

*

I am
learning to trust the rhythm of
my own feelings.

*

Feelings are like the weather

Feelings are like the weather, constantly shifting and changing—sometimes dark, sometimes light, at times wild and intense, at other times calm and quiet. Trying to resist your feeling experience is like trying to control the weather—an exercise in futility and frustration! Besides, if all we ever experienced were sunny days of exactly 75-degree temperature, life might become boring after a while. When we can appreciate the beauty of the rain, the wind, and the snow as well as the sun, then we will be free to experience the fullness of life.

*

*I accept and
appreciate all the varieties of
my internal "weather."*

*

You can't change your emotions
through will

The mental level and the emotional level function quite differently. On a mental level, you can exercise a certain degree of control. You can choose to focus your thoughts in a certain way for a given period of time, which can make a difference in your life. But you can't change your emotions through will. Emotions don't have anything to do with will. What you can do with emotions is accept them, experience them, and express them. That's the key to dealing with emotions. It's fine to change your thoughts, but it's not fine to try to change your emotions.

*

I *am*
learning to feel and express my
emotions.

*

You can't force yourself
to feel a certain way

The biggest misunderstanding about joy, love, and the "positive" feelings is the idea that you can be joyful or filled with love by *trying* to be or *wanting* to be. People try to go directly to those experiences. They don't want to feel sad or fearful; they just want to feel joyful and loving.

Unfortunately, you can't truly get any feeling by trying to do it or wanting to do it. Love and joy are the natural results of letting yourself feel all your emotions fully, healing your emotional wounds, and accepting and expressing all aspects of yourself.

*

Love and joy are
the natural results of accepting
all my other feelings.

*

There are no negative feelings

There's no such thing as a negative feeling. The feelings we call negative are the ones we are afraid to allow ourselves to experience. All feelings are simply a natural part of life. They have a natural function in our lives. If we allow ourselves to feel them as they happen, we learn something from the experience and they pass through rather quickly.

If we try to avoid, repress, or deny a feeling, it gets stuck. It gains tremendous power and blocks us from feeling anything else. Each time we try to avoid feeling a so-called negative emotion, we shut ourselves down a little more. In this way, we deny ourselves the positive feelings, too.

*

I allow
myself to experience all
my feelings.

*

To experience joy,
feel your sadness

If you want to experience more joy in your life, you need to be willing to fully experience your sadness when it comes. If you are holding sadness inside, you will carry a heavy feeling around with you, and your attempts to be happy and enjoy life will feel superficial. If you have old sadness that you've never allowed yourself to experience, let yourself move into the emotion. Tears are the river of life, bathing our wounds and washing away our pain. Feeling our sadness allows our hearts to open so we can love and be loved. Joy is the inevitable result of allowing the river of life to flow freely through us.

*

I *am*
willing to feel my sadness
and my joy.

*

Allow yourself to grieve

Grief is an emotion we feel when we lose someone or something we love. It's vitally important to allow yourself to grieve when you suffer any loss in your life—major or minor. Once you have freely experienced and expressed your grief in a given moment, you will experience a feeling of inner peace. Grief comes in waves, so you may have to go through this cycle many times. For a serious loss, such as the death of a loved one or the ending of an important relationship, the waves may come at less and less frequent intervals for years. Allowing your full grieving process enables you to gradually release the old and open to all the new wonders that are coming into your life.

*

*I allow
myself to grieve my losses. Gradually,
in my own time, I release the old
and welcome the new.*

*

To experience love,
you must feel your own anger

If you want to feel more love, you must allow yourself to feel your anger. If you are afraid of anger, find a good therapist (who's not afraid of anger!) to help you learn safe, constructive ways to experience and express anger. Underneath anger, there is always some way you've been hurt or some way you've given your power away. When you uncover and express the hurt, the healing can take place. When you learn to assert your needs and feelings directly, you'll feel less anger. Eventually you will feel love and compassion toward the person you were angry at.

Our natural state is love when it is not blocked by repressed emotions. Our spirits automatically feel love. When we embrace and make peace with our own feelings, we will recognize the being in others and feel love for them.

*

I am learning to
feel and express my anger appropriately
and constructively.

*

Feelings are physical, too

Every time you don't allow yourself or you aren't allowed to fully experience an emotion, to feel it, and to move through it, the energy of that emotion becomes stopped and blocked in your body. It remains until you can go back and reexperience that emotion. Then the energetic block is released and the body is freed and cleared. Virtually all our physical ailments come from energetic blocks in our bodies, energetic patterns that are connected to our emotional patterns.

*

*I am feeling
and releasing all emotional energies
in my body.*

*

Respect your fear

Many people want to get over being afraid or want to get rid of fear, because they see their fear as holding them back from what they really want: confidence, expansion, and freedom.

But, like everything, fear needs to be respected and honored as a part of our experience. It's there for a reason and is a necessary part of life. It's not to be gotten rid of; it's to be acknowledged and worked with. We needn't fear our fear! We could modify Franklin Roosevelt's statement to "The only thing we have to fear is fear of fear itself."

*

*I am learning
to acknowledge and respect
my own fears.*

*

Fear can be appropriate

Fear and love are the emotions that correspond with the two metaphysical principles of contraction and expansion. Fear is basically contraction. It's a pulling back or a contracting away from. It can be a very appropriate feeling. When you touch something hot, your body contracts to keep you from hurting yourself. The natural and appropriate function of fear is to cause you to be somewhat contracted and to approach a situation with caution until you understand or see what it is or how to handle it correctly and safely.

*

What are my fears?
Might there be an appropriate warning
in some of them?

*

We have many inner selves

Most of us think we're supposed to be one consistent personality, and we wonder why we sometimes feel so inconsistent. One day we feel one way; another day we feel another way. Sometimes one minute we feel one thing, and the next minute we feel something quite different.

We actually have many people within us, many different characters. We can think of these different parts as subpersonalities, or selves, or different voices within our personalities. To understand our own inner conflicts and inconsistencies, we need to get to know these inner selves.

*

I *am*
discovering my many inner
selves.

*

*The most important step
is awareness*

The process of consciousness involves getting to know our many inner selves and bringing them into balance and integration in our personalities and in our lives. The most important and most difficult step is to become aware of them and recognize them as individual voices. As we develop this awareness, we are no longer unconsciously run by whichever self happens to be in control at a given moment. We now have real, conscious choice in our lives.

*

I *am
becoming aware of my
inner voices.*

*

Each self has its own perspective

Each of our subpersonalities has its own set of needs and desires, its own point of view, its own opinions. Often they are diametrically opposed to one another. We may have a part of us, for example, that thinks that the most important thing to do is work very hard and become successful. And if that part of us is unconsciously running the show, we will be working all the time. On the other hand, there is an opposite self who just wants to relax, hang out, goof off, and enjoy life. Both voices are important, and each has value in our lives. Our job is to find the right balance between the two.

*

I am finding
balance between my opposite
parts.

*

Primary selves and disowned selves

We become strongly identified with certain subpersonalities; these are the ones we unconsciously allow to run our lives and to make our decisions. These are called our primary selves. The opposite subpersonalities are often repressed or undeveloped. These are called our disowned selves.

For example, your primary selves might be organized and orderly and like to plan ahead; your disowned selves might be creative, chaotic, and spontaneous (or vice versa). Perhaps your primary selves are laid back and relaxed, and you've disowned your aggressive, goal-oriented side (or vice versa). Your primary selves might be serious and responsible and your disowned energies playful and carefree.

*

What are my primary selves?
What are my more disowned
selves?

*

Balance

As you become more aware of your primary selves, you will no longer be unconsciously identified with them. You will notice that you start to open up more to your disowned selves. Other sides of you will start coming out to claim more space in your life.

You will find greater balance coming into every aspect of your life as you allow this process to happen naturally.

*

*Greater balance
is coming into every aspect
of my life.*

*

Respect all of your selves

Each of the people inside us, our various selves, is an essential part of us. It's very important to get to know and to respect them all. Each is an aspect of our personality that we need to learn to know, respect, explore, and appreciate. By allowing ourselves to know and express *all* the subpersonalities within us, we can become balanced instead of being identified with only one side of a polarity. Ideally we want to explore both sides of every polarity and then be able to choose the appropriate moments for the different selves to come forth.

*

I am learning
to respect and appreciate all my selves
as I explore and get to
know them.

*

Every voice is important

Some of our inner selves may be difficult for us to accept at first. For example, we might feel upset to discover that there's an angry voice inside. Because it's been suppressed and ignored all our lives, it's become even angrier. It's never been listened to and hasn't had a chance to have its feelings heard. We can start to find safe, comfortable, appropriate ways to allow our anger to be experienced and expressed. Underneath the anger we will find an assertive self that is trying to take care of us by standing up for us, setting boundaries and asking for what we need. This is an important voice that needs to be part of our lives.

*

I accept
all of my inner
voices.

*

Every self offers a gift

Each inner character has a place in our lives and each has a gift to give us. There's no part of us that's essentially bad. If you are identified with a sub-personality that loves to give to others, you may have disowned your selfish side because you think that that part of you is bad. Yet, without it you may become a self-sacrificing martyr or one who cares for others but not yourself. Being aware of the part of you that's concerned with your inner needs will not make you a selfish person. It will help you take responsibility for getting your needs met and thereby bring you balance. We must know, accept, and love all aspects of ourselves so that we can use and appreciate each gift.

*

I am learning
to recognize the gift each self has
to offer me.

*

*Think of your selves
as a family*

In getting to know all your inner selves, you might think of them as being your inner family. As in most families, there's a certain amount of conflict and there's also a lot of love. Let every member of your inner family play its role, express itself, and be respected for the part it plays in the family, so that ultimately the family can be in harmony.

*

*I apreciate
and respect each member of
my own inner "family."*

*

Think of your selves
as a committee

Another interesting metaphor for your inner selves is to think of them as a committee. When you think about yourself as a committee, it often explains why it is so difficult for you to make a decision or finish a job. We all know what happens when a decision is made by a committee. One person wants one thing, another wants something else, and all too often nothing gets done. If you can get to know the members of your inner committee and allow them to express themselves clearly, then *you*, as a conscious person, can begin to make the decisions instead of allowing whichever part of you happens to grab control in any given moment make the decisions.

*

I allow
each member of my committee
to be heard; then I make
the decision.

*

The protector-controller

Many of our subpersonalities are defense mechanisms we have developed to help us survive in the world. For example, our protector-controller is a conservative voice that tries to protect us by making sure we follow the proper rules and behave in an appropriate way that will not threaten our security. This is the part of us that resists growth and change because it feels safer doing things the way we've always done them. It needs to be gently reassured that the changes we're making are not foolish or dangerous.

*

It's safe
for me to grow and
change.

*

The pleaser

The pleaser is a part of our psyche that wants to make sure we always behave in a way that makes everyone like us, approve of us, and never be upset with us. It's an expert at finding out what other people want and trying to give it to them. The pleaser would do anything for love and approval. Unfortunately, it keeps us from expressing our real feelings and thoughts if it suspects someone important might disagree or be upset. The more we learn to love and approve of ourselves, the less anxious the pleaser will be about what everyone else thinks.

*

I *love*
and approve of
myself.

*

The perfectionist

Many of us have the idea that perfection is an attainable goal. We believe this because we have a strong inner voice called the perfectionist. The perfectionist's job is to set incredibly high standards for everything about us: our appearance, our behavior, our work, and anything else we are concerned with in life. Our perfectionist voice can point us in a positive direction. But it may set such high standards that it's impossible to attain them. We can appreciate our inner perfectionist for its well-meaning attempt to make us perfect, but we must stop expecting ourselves to achieve the impossible!

*

*I don't need
to try to be perfect. I accept myself
as I am.*

*

The perfectionist seeks love

The inner perfectionist comes from our childhood. We hope that if we can live up to some high standard we will get the love, appreciation, and validation we didn't get during childhood. We need to become conscious of the goals of the perfectionist that we have been striving so hard to please. Then we can choose goals and standards that are more realistic and appropriate, and learn to love ourselves for who we are.

*

I love myself
as I am now. I choose goals that
are realistic and
attainable.

*

The pusher

Our inner pusher drives us to accomplish as much as we can. The pusher loves to make lists of tasks and feels that the most important thing in life is getting it all done. Like the perfectionist, it is unaware that what it's asking for is impossible. It has no perspective on other things that may be important in our lives, such as relaxation or intimacy. The pusher is strongly reinforced by our cultural emphasis on productivity and accomplishment.

Becoming conscious of your inner pusher and achieving some separation from it can change your life dramatically.

*

I am
letting go of pushing myself.
I can achieve my goals in life
in a relaxed way.

*

The inner critic

The inner critic is the voice that keeps us constantly informed of what we are doing wrong; how we have fallen short; what mistakes we have made, are currently making, and will probably make in the future; how terrible our appearance is; and generally how inadequate we are! Many people's lives are unconsciously run by their critics (or a combination of perfectionist-pusher-critic). It is a great relief to begin to get some awareness and separation from our critics and to realize that most of what our critics tell us is not necessarily true.

*

*There is
nothing wrong with
me!*

*

The inner critic tries
to protect you

The function of the inner critic is to protect the child from behaving in ways that will incur criticism, attack, punishment, rejection, or abandonment from outside. The critic was born from the process of receiving criticism in childhood. Whatever our parents, other authority figures, siblings, or peers criticized us for was incorporated into our inner critic. As an adult, it's no longer appropriate or necessary for our inner critic to have control over us. A harsh inner critic who constantly tells us what's wrong with us and how inadequate we are perpetuates low self-esteem and lack of confidence.

It's time to become conscious of your critic so it doesn't automatically run your life anymore. It takes time to heal the inner critic, but it can be done, and it will make a wonderful difference in your life!

*

I *am*
becoming conscious of my
inner critic.

*

Healing the inner critic

Healing the inner critic is challenging. It doesn't help to try to shut it up; it will just become stronger. The key is consciousness. The first step is to recognize its voice, to begin to notice what it says to you, and to begin to get in touch with where it came from in your childhood. When you recognize it as only a voice instead of an absolute truth, you are becoming conscious. Then you can ask yourself, "Is this true? Do I need to believe this? Do I have to let this stop me or run my life?"

Underneath the negativity, the critic often has a grain of truth or a valid point. Let the critic know that you appreciate its point of view, but that you will no longer be run by criticism.

*

*I am
healing my inner
critic.*

*

The healthy inner critic

The essential function of the inner critic is discrimination: what's appropriate, what's not appropriate, what's better, what's worse. We need to have that perspective. To live in society, we need to understand what kinds of results our behavior will incur and make appropriate choices. A healthy, functioning, critical faculty inside ourselves would say things like, "You look better in this dress than you do in that one," or "The speech you gave yesterday could be improved by doing the following things." In other words, it's that part of our minds that can recognize ways to improve, but it doesn't have a heavily judgmental quality. It's our ability to learn from what we do and to make useful distinctions among behaviors.

*

I am learning
to discriminate rather than
to criticize.

*

Cultivate a positive voice

As you become aware of your inner critic, start cultivating an opposite voice. This voice doesn't have to get rid of the critic. It can help to balance the critic's voice by providing support and encouragement. It can be a positive parental voice that says, "Hey, you're doing great. Look how much progress you've made. You're a worthy, lovable person." Saying affirmations is one way of cultivating a positive inner voice that counteracts the negative messages your critic gives you. Affirmations can be very powerful, especially if used regularly.

*

I am learning
to give myself support and
encouragement.

*

*
**

Spring

**
*

Take fun seriously!

If you are completely hedonistic, searching only for pleasure and enjoyment, your life will feel meaningless. On the other hand, if you take life too seriously and deprive yourself of fun and enjoyment, it will feel just as empty. The key is to balance seriousness and fun.

When you are seriously dedicated to a path of consciousness, it can be hard to remember to have fun. So take fun seriously! Make it important! Think of it as one of those essentials you must include in your life regularly. Think about what things are fun for you. What do you enjoy? What makes you laugh? What makes you feel good? Do at least one fun thing every day.

*

Today,
and every day,
I do at least one thing just
for fun.

*

The inner child

One of the most important parts of ourselves to get to know is our inner child. The child lives inside each of us, always. In fact, we have the energies of many different child selves within us. We have a child for every age we've been, from infancy through adolescence. And our inner child has many aspects. The child carries our sensitivity, our feelings, our creativity, and many other important qualities.

*

I am getting
to know my inner child in all its
many aspects.

*

The inner child is buried

The spiritual essence comes into the human form and is born as a child. Because the child is extremely sensitive and vulnerable and the world is not a very safe or comfortable environment for it, the child immediately begins to develop defense and survival mechanisms—behaviors to protect itself and get its needs met. These mechanisms become the different selves, or subpersonalities, and together form the structure of the personality.

Eventually, the child and the spiritual essence within it become buried underneath the complex and rigid personality structure that's trying to protect it. So we unconsciously live out our defenses and survival mechanisms, and forget that the reason we have them in the first place is to take care of and fulfill the needs of the child.

*

I
*recognize the child deep
within me.*

*

The vulnerable child

The vulnerable child is the emotional core of our being. It carries all our deepest feelings and is extremely sensitive, very loving, and easily hurt or frightened. It lives deep inside us, and whether or not we are aware, it is constantly reacting to everything that happens to us according to whether it feels safe and loved or threatened, rejected, or abandoned. It needs a great deal of love, nurturing, and reassurance. Often our vulnerable child has been wounded through various life experiences and needs special attention and healing.

*

I am loving
and healing my vulnerable
child.

*

The playful child

The playful child is the part of us that knows how to have fun. It loves to play and laugh and is always on the lookout for ways to have a good time. Some adults have managed to stay in touch with their playful child; they are the ones who know how to enjoy themselves. But most of us, as we've grown into adulthood, have disowned our playful child. Without it, life feels dull and drab. We need to reconnect with our natural, playful inner child who adds sparkle to our lives.

*

I *love*
to play and have
fun.

*

The magical child

We also have a magical child inside us. It's the part of us that's naturally tuned in to the unseen energies of the universe. It loves to be in nature, where it can relate to the spirits of plants and animals, and perhaps to elves and fairies. The magical child loves to daydream, imagine, and fantasize. It likes special implements, like magic wands and crystals. As adults, we've disowned this child because we fear that it's foolish and silly. To get back in touch with that magical child can be an incredible experience. It puts wonder and amazement back in our lives, because life *is* magic.

*

I *feel*
the wonder and magic
of life.

*

The wise child

Another aspect of our inner child is the wise child. It's the part of us that's very truthful, that sees and knows what we're feeling and what others are feeling. It has the power to cut through much of the superficial dishonesty that exists in adult society, and always goes right to the core truth of situations. This child has usually been buried because we were taught to believe in the denial all around us. If we can reclaim this part of ourselves, we can connect to a tremendous source of wisdom.

*

*I am learning
to trust my wise inner
child.*

*

Make it safe for your
inner child to come out

In order to allow your inner child to come out, you must first deal with the voices in you that really don't like the child or are afraid of the child—the parts of you that don't want the child to come out. Honor those parts of you. They are some of your primary selves. Your primary selves have been running your life until now. They deserve a lot of respect because they have gotten you this far. They've made you as successful as you are. They provided safety and they helped you survive. Recognize their reasons for being. Those parts of you are uncomfortable with the inner child because it hasn't been safe to be vulnerable in this world.

Instead of fighting those parts of yourself and making them wrong, respect and appreciate them.

*

I honor the parts
of myself that have hidden
my inner child.

*

Our protector selves fear emotions

Our rational, parental, primary selves have learned to protect the child in us by staying away from anything that may potentially be emotional or traumatic. Their idea about how to take care of the inner child is to bury it underground and keep all feelings suppressed. They become very anxious about exploring feelings because emotions make them feel out of control. Their philosophy is to just keep doing what's worked so far. Why risk changing when they've survived until now? Don't rock the boat because any kind of change could be a potential disaster.

It's true that those parts of ourselves have helped us survive. But they have also cut us off from our very human needs and emotions. We need to acknowledge their fears and concerns, and gently reassure them that it's safe now to begin to explore and express our feelings.

*

It's safe
to feel and express
my emotions.

*

Cultivate your conscious adult

As you cultivate your conscious adult self, you begin to take over the job that your primary selves have been doing. The primary selves have been unconsciously protecting and parenting the inner child the only way they knew how. Becoming aware of that process and making conscious choices to parent and care for your inner child relieves the burden of the primary selves, and they can let go and relax a little.

*

I am becoming
a conscious adult who cares for
my inner child.

*

Reassure your inner protector

As a conscious adult you can now address that part of you that says, "Don't ever be vulnerable!" You can say, "I can see why it hasn't felt good to be vulnerable until now because it would have been pretty dangerous and scary. Don't worry, I won't be vulnerable in a way that's really stupid or foolish or is going to get me hurt. I'm going to make some conscious choices now. From time to time it will be okay for me to be vulnerable in situations when there's somebody who really cares about me. I'll check it out and make sure it's really safe. I'm going to start bringing that vulnerability out, but I'm not going to take it out and lay it in the middle of the street."

Continually reassure the protective part of you that's anxious because you are beginning to open up.

*

It's safe
for me to be vulnerable at
appropriate times.

*

We must fill the inner child's needs
appropriately

The inner child never goes away. It never grows up. It never dies. It is with us throughout our entire lives.

If we're not aware of our child's needs, then we are constantly trying to fulfill them unconsciously. The child within is unconsciously motivating all our behavior. We may, for example, develop a subpersonality that's a workaholic because it's trying to make enough money to make the child feel safe and protected. But we end up forgetting about the child and spend our whole lives working hard. We may accumulate a lot of money and success, but none of it gives us the satisfaction we need because we've forgotten about the child who was the original motivating force.

*

I am learning
to recognize and fill my inner child's
needs.

*

The inner child doesn't need wealth

Many people pursue wealth out of an unconscious need to provide security for their inner child. The child in us does need to have some sense of financial security, but only on a rather basic level. The child needs to know that it's going to have a safe, comfortable home, enough good food to eat, some comfortable, attractive clothes to wear, and the opportunity to learn and grow and create. That's all the child needs in terms of financial security. Beyond that, the child needs love, companionship, appropriate boundaries, emotional support, freedom of expression, and fun.

*

*I give
my inner child what it truly
needs.*

*

Money is not security

Many people have gotten safety and security mixed up with money. Most of us, to some degree, are motivated by fear when it comes to money. We feel that somehow money can give us security. Whether we have little money or a lot of money doesn't matter. We feel that if we could only have more, we would feel safe and secure. But underneath, we are basically trying to take care of our inner child. Money is a way of trying to make the child feel safe when we're not in touch with the child's real needs. But money is not necessarily what the child wants. We need to be in communication with the child and find out what the child really needs, and give it.

*

*What
does my inner child really
want?*

*

The inner child
can block success

Sometimes the inner child will actually sabotage our attempts to be successful or to do the things we think we should do, because secretly the child knows that its needs will not be met by what we're striving for. Often, when people have a block about being successful in life, the block comes from the inner child whose needs are not being met. The child may stop you from being professionally successful until you start to give it more nurturing, more love, more time to play, or whatever it needs.

*

I am giving my
inner child the love and attention
it needs.

*

Learn to care for the inner child

Our challenge is to get in touch with our inner child, to find out what the child's needs are, and to begin consciously to take care of the child. The child's needs are for love, for safety, for physical and emotional contact, for enjoyment, and to express itself honestly and creatively. As we begin to find ways of doing those things, we find that our whole personality starts to come into alignment and we become healthy and balanced.

*

I *am*
learning to contact my inner child
and to ask it what it
needs.

*

Learning to parent ourselves

Because most of us did not receive fully adequate parenting, we have not learned to parent our inner child effectively. The child inside feels unloved, unsupported, frightened, and needy. Unconsciously, we attempt to provide for that child through overeating, drinking, or using drugs; overworking; or other addictive or dysfunctional behaviors.

In order to take good care of ourselves we need to develop the ability to parent ourselves consciously and wisely, by discovering the true needs of our inner child and learning to provide them in a way that really works.

*

I *am*
learning to be a good parent
to myself.

*

Developing the inner mother
and father

To effectively parent our inner child in the world, we need to develop two functions: the ability to "mother" ourselves and the ability to "father" ourselves.

The inner mother is the nurturing aspect—the ability to give ourselves love, caring, compassion, understanding. We mother ourselves by being sensitive to our deepest needs and learning to fill them.

The inner father is the supportive, protective aspect—the ability to take care of ourselves in relation to the outside world. We father ourselves by making clear communications, setting boundaries, and supporting our deep feelings with action.

*

I am
a good mother and father
to myself.

*

Contact the inner child

To get in touch with the child inside yourself, it's important to create the most positive possible environment for the safety and comfort of the child. Find a place that feels very comfortable and private. You may want to have a blanket, a stuffed animal, or something else that will make your child feel welcome.

Close your eyes, relax, and imagine you are in a very beautiful, safe, natural environment. Imagine a small child there—the child that you once were. You may see an image of this child or just get a feeling of it. Let the child know that you care about it. Ask the child what it needs and wants from you, as an adult. The communication with the child may be in words, or it may be nonverbal. Let the child know that you want to make regular contact to begin a conscious relationship.

*

*I am beginning
to make regular contact with
my inner child.*

*

Accept your inner child's feelings

When you first get in touch with your vulnerable inner child, you may find that it is very emotional. It may be hurt, sad, or even angry and resentful. Sometimes it's hard to accept that your child is so upset. Remember that the child is in pain because it has been wounded. Also, it may be hurt that you have abandoned and ignored it all your life! Accept the child's feelings, and give it lots of love and understanding. That's all it's ever needed.

*

I
accept my inner child's
feelings.

*

Be patient and consistent

Sometimes when you first try to contact your inner child, nothing seems to happen. Be willing to be patient. Sometimes the child is not yet ready to trust you. The child may hold back until it knows that you really want this contact and that you're willing to be responsible and consistent with the contact.

If you have difficulty contacting your child through meditation, let it go and find other ways to include your child in your life.

*

I *am*
patient and consistent with my
inner child.

*

Many ways to contact the inner child

There are many ways to get in touch with the child inside us. We can contact the child through playing, dancing, singing, drawing, or painting. Being out in a beautiful, natural environment tends to open the space for the child to emerge. Oftentimes the inner child comes forth with animals, because children naturally love animals and feel attuned to them. Experiment with some of these things to find out what your child responds to.

*

*I'm finding
many ways to be with
my inner child.*

*

To reconnect with your inner child,
look at real children

A good way to start to get in touch with or become aware of the child within you is to look at real children. Children reflect the child inside us. When we look into an infant's eyes, we will often feel a profound connection. Or, when we see a child being very playful, it brings out the playful side of ourselves. Or a child will say something to us that's so profoundly wise we feel extremely moved by it. This child, it seems, knows more than we do. That is a reflection of the knowingness of our own inner child.

*

Through contact with
real children, I am reconnecting with
my own inner child.

*

What does your inner child
like to do?

What did you enjoy doing as a young child? Being outdoors? Being with people? Being alone? Playing games? Swinging on swings? Having pillow fights? Reading books? Going to the movies? Let your inner child come out and play. Allow yourself to do the things you enjoyed as a child that you haven't done for a while. Or do something that you always wanted to do but were forbidden to do, or thought you never could do as a child.

*

I do at least
one thing each day that I loved
to do or wanted to do
as a child.

*

Take time with your inner child

Start to think about things that are fun or that are nurturing for your inner child, and begin to include them in your life in a regular way. Every day or at least every couple of days, take some time, even if it's just a few minutes in the morning or evening, and find out what your child likes to do. Of course, the most important thing to the child is love and intimacy, so your child will guide you in finding more contact, closeness, friendship, and love with other people. But it's also important to include things that are fun for the child, like taking a bubble bath or riding a bike—things that really feed and nurture your inner child.

*

*I am
taking the time each day to find out
what my inner child likes
to do.*

*

The inner child will tell you
what it wants

If you're not sure what the needs of your inner child are or how best to take care of your child, simply ask. The child knows its own feelings, needs, and desires. So cultivate the habit of communicating with the child, asking what it needs and wants. Then do your best to fulfill your child's needs. You can't always do everything the child wants when it wants, but you should include its needs in your life, just as you would with a real child. Make them as much a priority as you can, and you will find that the rewards are great.

*

I pay attention
to the needs of my inner child
and do my best to
fulfill them.

*

Buy your inner child a toy

Take your inner child to the store, and let it pick out a toy. Let your adult self determine how much you can reasonably afford to spend (it doesn't need to be much), then let the child pick whatever it wants within that budget. Sometimes what the child wants may be something your adult self thinks is silly or stupid or tasteless. Don't allow your judgments to interfere with the child's choice. By giving the child what it wants you are telling it that you care about it, that it matters. You make it safe for the child to come out. Then you can begin to get to know it.

*

Today
I will buy my inner child a toy—
something he or she
really wants.

*

Protect your inner child
when it's appropriate

It's important to learn when it's not appropriate to bring your inner child out. In the middle of a business meeting is usually not the best time to have your child come out, for example. You can allow your child to stay home and play, by telling the child that you're going to work and that you'll be home later on. Be sure the child knows that you'll take some time to play when you get home.

Even though it may feel a little silly at first, consciously taking care of your inner child's needs will end up bringing much more balance, harmony, enjoyment, and fulfillment in your life.

*

I protect my inner child
and let it come out only when I know
it is safe.

*

The inner child is closest
to our spiritual essence

The child within us is one of the most vital aspects of ourselves to contact, because it is closest to our spiritual essence. We come into this world as spiritual beings, which are born into the physical body as infants. When the child is born it is almost purely spiritual essence, because at that point it has no contact or experience with the world. That is why we are so moved when we are with very young children; we see the reflection of our own profound, beautiful, and innocent spiritual essence that has not yet been buried or hidden.

*

As I *contact*
my inner child, I *open to my*
spiritual essence.

*

*The inner child connects us
with our souls*

It is so important to rediscover the inner child within each of us and allow it to express itself. As we discover the true feelings and needs of the child and begin to nurture and care for it consciously and effectively, we find that most of our old, rigid defense systems are no longer necessary and we begin to relax and let go. The child comes alive and brings us emotional depth and authenticity, spontaneity, innocence, and joy. Through the child we reconnect with our souls, the essence of our being. Once again we are in contact with the universal spirit, the oneness of all life.

*

*Through my inner child,
I am in contact with
my soul.*

*

The Earth is our mother

As our mother, the earth is our best teacher. If we pay attention, we can learn from her everything we need to know about how to live on the physical plane. Every day, in every way, she demonstrates to us her natural rhythms and cycles, all the natural laws of life.

*

*I am becoming
aware of the rhythms of life,
within myself and all
around me.*

*

Live with the rhythm
of the earth

The pressures of modern life tend to move us away from the natural cycles and rhythms of the earth. We get up when the alarm clock rings; we go to bed after the eleven o'clock news. Life is structured according to what we *think* needs to be done, not according to a natural rhythm. Yet, we are part of the earth. We need to acknowledge that, to respect the earth's rhythms and live in accordance with them.

*

I *am*
a part of the earth
and the earth is a part
of me.

*

The rhythms of the earth
affect us

We are not machines that can produce the same output each day. Our mental and emotional states are different on sunny summer days than they are on cloudy winter days. And there are myriad subtle changes each day that affect us. If we can acknowledge and accept these differences each day, we can move more in the flow of life.

*

I am noticing
how the condition of the earth
affects me.

*

Be outdoors

In order to get more in touch with our connection to the earth, it is essential to be outside each day, even for a few minutes. It is only by having that direct contact each day that we can become conscious of the subtle changes that are occurring through the seasons. Of course, if you live in a city it is a little more difficult, but almost everyone can walk outside, observe the sky, and feel the air and sun.

*

Each day
I spend time outdoors,
connecting with the earth and
with myself.

*

Find a special place

Find a natural place that you love that lets you be in touch with the earth. It should be a place that's easily accessible to you. If you live in a city and don't have much access to the outdoors, find a space that lets you at least see the sky and feel the sun. Spend some time in your special place as often as you can, preferably every day. Explore it, get to know it. Find a comfortable place there to relax and meditate. Imagine that you are tuning into the spirit of this place. Ask if it has anything to communicate to you. Ask for anything you would like to receive here, such as serenity, nurturing, healing, or personal power.

*

I love
spending time in my special place
on earth.

*

Find a power object

Go out in a beautiful natural setting and find a comfortable place to sit for a short meditation. Breathe deeply, relax your body and mind, and let your awareness drop into a deep, quiet place inside you. Ask your inner intuitive self to guide you to an appropriate power object. Then get up and take a leisurely walk, looking around you and observing everything you see on the ground and in your surroundings. Pick things up and look at them if you feel drawn to them. At some point you will find an object that feels meaningful or powerful to you. It could be anything—a rock, leaf, feather, sea shell, or pine cone.

Sit down and hold your power object. Ask it what meaning or significance it has for you. Then take it home and put it in a special place, preferably where you can see it and acknowledge it each day.

*

My power object
reminds me what I need
to remember.

*

Notice where you live

It is interesting to notice how our geographical location relates to our process of balancing our masculine and feminine polarities. Quiet, natural environments tend to support the female aspect of our being. Lively, active environments stimulate the male energy. Warmer temperatures help us to relax and open our receptive, feminine energies. Colder climates provide a physical challenge and promote hard work and focused attention, which develops our masculine side. So New York City is in many ways the ultimate expression of male energy; Hawaii is an example of an extremely feminine environment. Most places contain a range of elements in between those two extremes.

*

*I'm noticing
how my environment affects
my process.*

*

Become aware of
your environment

Think about the ways in which the geography of
where you live affects your life, both outwardly and
inwardly. Does it primarily support your evolution
or detract from it? What's right for you depends
on many personal factors—what life experiences
you've already had, what phase of life you are in,
what your goals are, and what aspects of your
personality need to be developed and strength-
ened. When you become aware of the effect your
physical location has on your personal process, you
can take steps to create more balance.

*

In what ways
does my physical environment support
my process? In what ways does it
detract from it?

*

Steps to create balance

If you live in a city, you may need to visit a park daily, spend weekends in the country, and/or take regular vacations to more serene environments. If you live in a rural environment, you may find that occasional trips to the city are a necessary form of stimulation. If you lead a sedentary life-style with a great deal of mental focus, you may need regular vacations to an environment that provides physical challenge and spiritual attunement, such as skiing or river rafting. And you may need to consider changing your place of residence to one that is more supportive to the current stage of your life's journey.

*

I *am*
creating positive change and
balance in my physical
environment.

*

We are animals, too

As human beings, we tend to identify with our mental energies, our rational intelligence that distinguishes us from animals. Yet, physically we are animals, too. We tend to disown our animal selves, but disowning separates us from our environment and prevents us from knowing how to live comfortably and naturally in our physical bodies. We need to reclaim the animal aspect of our nature. Our minds can be only as good as the physical selves that support them.

*

I honor
and respect my animal
side.

*

Animals can be our teachers

Our animal brothers and sisters have a great deal to teach us. Through relating to our domesticated animals or studying and observing wild animals, we can learn a lot about ourselves that we have forgotten. Animals are deeply connected to their essential beings. They express themselves freely and naturally through their physical forms. They instinctively follow the rhythms of life. They can help us learn to live comfortably and naturally on earth.

*

*Through observing
animals I can learn about
myself.*

*

Discover your power animal

Imagine you are walking through a forest or a jungle. You see or feel the presence of many animals around you. At some point you encounter an animal that has particular significance for you. Ask what its message is to you, and be open to receiving it. This animal may talk to you in words or telepathically, or it may indicate what it wants to say to you through its actions. Trust whatever intuitive feelings come to you, and relate to the animal accordingly.

This animal represents a certain kind of power or wisdom. Let yourself receive its special gift to you. Know that this animal is now your special friend or ally, and you can call on it whenever you need its energy.

*

My
power animal gives me
special strength.

*

Treasure your body

In our culture, we tend to ignore our physical bodies or take them for granted. We need to learn to acknowledge and appreciate our bodies for all they do for us.

Every day, be with your physical body in ways that feel good. This does not mean making it do things that you *think* are good for it. Let your body do things that actually feel fulfilling, fun, enlivening, pleasurable. Be outdoors, walk, breathe, dance, swim, rest, listen to beautiful music, get a massage, eat delicious nourishing food. Let your body enjoy itself!

*

Every day,
I am doing something
that feels good to my body.

*

Find your own rhythm

Our physical bodies have certain basic requirements: sleep, nourishment, physical activity, fresh
air. We need to fulfill these requirements in a
regular rhythm. We sleep better if we go to bed at a
regular time each night and awake at the same time
each morning. It adds to our well-being if we eat and
exercise with a certain regularity. We need to discover and honor our own natural physical rhythms.

*

I *appreciate*
and care for my body in its
own rhythm.

*

Daily habits

Begin to get a sense of your physical requirements. Start noticing when your preferred time is to wake up or to go to bed. Notice when you get the most energy from eating. When is the best time for you to exercise? It's important to set up the best rhythm for yourself, one that you can fulfill each day. If you find yourself not able to adhere to the same rhythm, it is probably not right for you. Keep exploring until you find the rhythm that works for you.

*

Every day
I wake, eat, exercise, and sleep
in a way that makes me feel good and
filled with energy.

*

Awakening your body

When you wake up each morning, lie in bed for a few minutes and tune in to how your body is feeling. Tell your body that you appreciate it for being there for you. Stretch and move your body in a way that feels good. Slowly get up. Drink a large glass of water, and think about how the water is cleansing and re-plenishing your body. Don't drink or eat anything else for a few minutes. Allow yourself to connect with the natural energy of your body before starting the activities of the day.

*

Each morning
I take a little time to be
aware of my body.

*

Breathe

Every day, preferably just after you get up, take a few slow, deep breaths. Breathe fully, so that you feel both your chest and your stomach expand. As you exhale, think about releasing old patterns and limitations that you no longer need in your life. As you inhale, think about breathing in new life, health, and energy.

*

I exhale whatever
I no longer need. I inhale everything I now
need and want.

*

Nourish your body

It's important to find the right daily rhythm to nourish your body with food. Every body has slightly different needs, so tune into what your own body is telling you. The traditional three daily meals may not work for you. Some people find light snacking through the morning and two large meals later in the day satisfying. Some people want a heavy meal in the middle of the day and then a light supper. Some people want an energy boost at four o'clock, between lunch and dinner. Pay attention to how your body responds to the food you give it, and modify your schedule accordingly.

*

I *nourish*
my body in a way that fills me
with energy.

*

Exercise

Every day, move and stimulate your body in a way that is energizing and fun. To fulfill your body's daily requirements, it is not necessary to exercise to the point of pain. A daily walk is enough for most people. Or you can swim, do yoga or stretching exercises, attend a regular aerobics class, bicycle, or play some sport that you enjoy, like basketball or tennis. Be careful not to push your body too far. Balance strenuous exertion with more moderate exercise like stretching or walking.

*

Every day
I exercise my body
in a way that is stimulating
and fun.

*

Sleep

How much sleep do you get each night? Do you habitually keep yourself going during the day with coffee or other stimulants? In our left-brained, active, producing society, we often push ourselves continuously and don't give ourselves enough time to rest. The human body needs rest and sleep in order to function. Let yourself sleep as long as you need to.

*

I *give*
myself the sleep I need
each night.

*

Listen to your body

Any time your body is ailing, your spirit is trying to communicate something to you. Your spirit is telling you that you need to become conscious of something. Ask your body what it's trying to tell you.

The body is very literal. It will show you as graphically as it can what you need to be aware of, which always has to do with taking better care of yourself and loving yourself more.

*

I listen
to what my body is
telling me.

*

The emotional and physical
work together

Healing the emotional level is closely connected
with integrating and healing the physical level. In
the process of doing emotional healing work we
usually also have to do physical healing—through
massage and body work, various forms of alternative healing like chiropractic or acupuncture, or
working with diet and nutrition. We can accomplish
tremendous healing through movement, dance,
exercise—letting the energy of life flow through
our bodies.

We have to physically clear out the places where
energy has been blocked in our bodies, which is
usually connected with our emotional experiences.
It speeds up the process of healing to work on both
physical and emotional levels simultaneously.

*

My physical
and emotional healing processes
work together. Each supports
the other.

*

Touch is vital

Think of how litters of kittens or litters of puppies all pile up and snuggle together. We humans long for close physical contact, too. In most societies, until recently, families lived in much closer physical contact. But our society is not open about touching.

Touch and closeness are nourishing, soothing, and comforting to the child in us and are a vital element in life. We have divorced ourselves from that. Not only do we not touch each other, but we live in separate rooms and separate houses in what can really amount to a very lonely existence.

*

Each day
I physically touch someone
in a way that feels nourishing to both
of us.

*

We need community

The way our society is now set up separates most of us from the kind of emotional and social contact we need. We need to consciously take steps, if possible, to change our living conditions so that they're more conducive to sharing and to a sense of family, or tribe, or connectedness to other people. And if we can't actually change our living conditions, then we need to reach out and form connections and bonds with other people in our community.

*

I'm creating
a sense of community in
my life.

*

All things are connected

Whatever befalls the earth befalls all of us. We all breathe the same air, we walk the same ground. If we spit upon the ground, we spit upon ourselves. Water flows into the sea, then is taken back into the air, then rains on all of us. The earth is our mother. Animals are our brothers and sisters.[1] We are all connected—the family of earth.

[1] I am paraphrasing the beautiful words of Chief Seattle of the Suwamish tribe in a letter to President Franklin Pierce.

*

*I feel connected
to everyone and everything
on earth.*

*

*Feel the life force
within you*

At one time, it was natural for us to feel a sense of deep oneness with life. As we became more and more civilized and industrialized, we lost touch with that feeling. Now, as individuals, as a culture, and worldwide in our mass consciousness, we are turning back toward it. We are beginning to recognize again that we are a part of the universe and that the life force within us connects us to one another and to every other living thing.

*

*The life force
within me connects me to everyone
and everything.*

*

We are made up of
the four elements

Our bodies, and all of creation, are made up of four elements: earth, air, fire, and water. Let yourself be conscious of all these elements, inside you and all around you. Earth is strong, steady, serene, and supportive. Water is flowing and swirling. Air is light and free, almost without form. Fire is heat, bright and energetic.

At different times we go through different phases of these elements. One day we may feel very light and airy, another time we will be filled with fire. Understand that these are all necessary phases, and we pass from one to the other.

*

I *am*
earth, air, fire, and
water.

*

Tree meditation

Find a special tree. Sit under it, or climb up and sit in it, or stand close to it and put your arms around it, finding whatever way feels right to relate to it physically.

Close your eyes and relax into a meditative state of mind. Imagine that this tree is a mother, father, brother, or sister to you. Talk to it in your mind and tell it how you feel about it. Then let your mind be quiet, and let yourself receive the energy from this tree. You may find it to be nurturing, or strong, or wise, or perhaps humorous. Trust whatever relationship you feel with this tree.

If you live nearby, come to see your tree often. You may find it to be a very comforting and loving friend.

*

I *have*
many kinds of friends
in this world.

*

Rock meditation

Find a big rock that's smooth enough to sit on, lie on, or lean against. Relax deeply and feel your body against the rock. Feel how strong and firm the rock is. Notice how cool or warm it is. Think about how ancient it is and how long it has been in this spot. Pretend you are the rock and try to imagine what it would be like to sit so calmly and still for hundreds, thousands, or perhaps millions of years. Let yourself absorb the serene, powerful energy of this rock.

*

*I feel the energy
of the earth through
this ancient rock.*

*

Ask for a blessing

Whenever you do anything in nature or related to the earth, take a moment to ask for a blessing from the earth and from the plant, animal, and other nature spirits in that place. Remember that we can never truly own a part of the earth. We are the caretakers, and the place will let us know what it needs and wants.

*

I am
a caretaker for the
earth.

*

Thank the earth

Each day when you get up, take a moment to look out your window or walk out into your yard and observe the beauty of nature as it is that day. If you live in a city apartment with no yard or trees, you can do this with your houseplants, or lean out a window and look at the sky.

Say thank you to the earth mother and to all the elements. Give thanks for another day of life. It is a precious gift.

*

I *give thanks*
for another beautiful day
on earth.

*

*Look at your life
as a reflection*

We create everything that happens to us. We attract or we are attracted to the people, events, and experiences that we need for our growth.

See in everything and everyone that you encounter, and every experience that you have, that it is a reflection of what's going on inside you. Then you can begin to correct the problems you are having in your relationship to yourself. You can begin to change. You can begin to heal the parts that don't work. And you can begin to expand and express and allow the things that are working best for you to come forth.

*

*I see my life
as a reflection of my inner
process.*

*

Our most important relationship

There's one relationship in our lives that's most important. It's the foundation of all our other relationships. And when that relationship is working, then all the other relationships in our lives work. When it isn't working, then none of the rest of our relationships do. That relationship is with ourselves.

If we focus on that inner relationship, we can see that everything else in our lives reflects how we feel about and treat ourselves. Through this awareness we can create more truthful, real, fulfilling, and powerful relationships with others.

*

*I am building
an honest, loving relationship
with myself and with
others.*

*

Wholeness is within us

Most of us have lost our relationship with ourselves. Out of the emptiness, loneliness, and desperation we feel because we've lost that connection inside ourselves we yearn to find fulfillment outside ourselves. We look for relationships, hoping we can find someone who can make us feel whole. But it doesn't happen.

No one else can fulfill you if you don't begin to develop the relationship with yourself. The primary connection is within. Wholeness is the experience of integrating and expressing all the many aspects of yourself.

*

*I am
finding wholeness within
myself.*

*

Bring spirit into the world

In the traditions of both East and West, those wishing to follow a spiritual path have withdrawn from the world, have become celibate, and have avoided intimate relationships. They view relationships as a distraction from the primary focus of spiritual development. In truth, it is difficult to stay consciously connected with our spiritual essence while we are dealing with the problems of worldly life and particularly the difficulties of relationships.

Yet, it is now time to move to a new level of spiritual practice. Now we must meet the challenge of bringing our spirit fully into the physical world, into every aspect and every moment of our daily lives. To do this, we must be willing to confront every issue that we might have avoided by removing ourselves from the world.

*

*I am bringing
my spiritual essence into my
daily life.*

*

We can't avoid relationships

There are times in our lives when it's appropriate to withdraw from the world and just focus on our relationship with ourselves. But, if we truly want to become conscious beings, we can't avoid relationships. Eventually we have to move into the world and use our relationships with everyone and everything around us to reflect our own inner process. They are the best mirror we have in which to clearly see ourselves. There is absolutely no learning that is not present in our relationships. They will literally teach us everything we need to know.

*

*My relationships
are teaching me what I need
to know.*

*

*Through our relationships
we can see ourselves*

It's much harder to look inside ourselves than it is to look at the outside world. That's why it's important to look at relationships as mirrors of what's going on inside us. We really can't see into ourselves very well. We can't see what we're unconscious of. But if we can look at our relationships and see that what they are reflecting is us, then we can begin to see ourselves.

*

*I see
myself mirrored in my
relationships.*

*

Relationship is our most
powerful tool

Relationship is probably the most powerful spiritual path that exists in the world today. It's the greatest tool that we have. Our relationships can be the fastest and the most powerful route to the deepest truths, if we know how to use them. This is true not only of our romantic relationships but also of every kind of relationship. This practice turns every moment of our lives into a meditation, into a workshop, into a creative possibility.

*

I am
learning from every relationship
in my life.

*

All energies need expression

The universe contains certain basic archetypes or patterns of energy. As individuals, we each potentially contain all of these archetypes. Generally we have developed some of them and those are the ones we identify with and express in our lives. The other energies are undeveloped or disowned, but are constantly seeking expression. In order to become balanced and whole, we must gradually learn to express all of these energies in our personalities and our lives. In a close relationship with another person, that person will usually start expressing the energies that we have disowned. In a family, anything that's not being expressed by either of the parents will start being expressed by one of the children. When you become conscious of this process, you can use all your relationships as mirrors to see what energies in you need more expression.

*

What energy
am I not expressing fully in my life?
How is that being reflected to me
in my relationships?

*

We have a wide range of energies

Every one of us has a much wider range of energies than we're aware of. Take a look at what it is about yourself that you reject or that you don't express. Life is trying to show you how you can begin to get in touch with those parts of yourself. One way life shows you that is through mirroring. The people you have in your life that you like and get along with easily, that you admire and appreciate and are fairly harmonious with, reflect the aspects of yourself that you like, that you have integrated into your being. The people in your life that you don't like, that give you trouble, that bug you, that you have judgments about, that you can't stand—those people mirror aspects of yourself that you have not learned to love, to integrate, to express in yourself.

*

Who is it
that I have problems with?
Can I see something in them that I am not
accepting in myself?

*

Opposites attract

Oftentimes we find ourselves attracted to and attracting our opposites—people who have developed opposite qualities from the ones that we are most identified with. We are unconsciously seeking to become whole, so we are attracted toward people who carry and express the energies that are undeveloped in our own personalities. On some level we recognize that they have the potential to help us become more balanced.

*

Who in my life
carries some opposite energies
from me?

*

They are our teachers

The people in our lives who carry our opposite energies can be our most powerful teachers if we allow them to be. We must recognize that they express those opposite polarities that we want and need. Early in a relationship, we often sense that the other person is bringing us exactly what we need. It is, in fact, their differentness that is so attractive to us. After a while, though, we begin to resent them for the way they are different and we try to change them to be more like us!

We must remember that we brought them into our lives to teach and inspire us. Our challenge is to be open to discovering the parts of ourselves that are mirrored by them.

*

The people
who are in relationship with me
are my teachers.

*

The messy versus neat polarity

One very common relationship problem is the conflict between order and spontaneity. Almost any two people who live together get into this polarization—one of them is neat and one of them is messy. It's really the conflict between that very structured, organized, linear side of ourselves and the more spontaneous, intuitive, and creative aspect of ourselves. One person is playing out one and the other is playing out the other.

You can have endless conflict between you until you recognize that the conflict is showing you that you need both parts. You each need to learn to find a balance and live in the balance between those two extremes.

*

I'm finding
the balance between order and spontaneity
in my life.

*

The commitment versus freedom polarity

It is very common in a relationship for one person to want greater commitment, greater depth, and greater intimacy and the other to want more freedom, more space. This outer conflict mirrors the conflicting polarities inside each of us. We all want closeness and intimacy and commitment. At the same time, we fear loss of freedom and individuality. If you have this type of conflict in a relationship, look to see what it might represent about those parts of yourself.

*

I can find
the freedom to be myself
within the commitment of a close
relationship.

*

The emotional/rational polarity

One conflict that comes up frequently in relationships is that one person tends to take a more
rational approach to life and to be more emotionally detached, and the other person tends to
take an emotional approach. Very frequently it
happens that that's a male/female polarity. Traditionally, men have been conditioned by society
to be more rational and women have been conditioned to be more emotional.

So, for example, if a very emotional woman is
with a very rational man, the man is being shown by
this woman that he needs to get more in touch with
his emotions and his feelings. And the woman is
being shown by the man that she needs to begin to
cultivate a more impersonal or detached energy
that would give her a certain kind of strength and
balance in her life.

*

*I'm finding
the balance of reason and
emotion.*

*

*We need to integrate
our opposite*

When there is an area of conflict in a relationship, it is usually a sign that each person is reflecting to the other one an energy that the other one needs to develop. If the two people don't begin to integrate these opposite energies, they will begin to polarize even further in their familiar directions.

For example, in the emotional/rational polarity, the woman will begin carrying the man's emotional energy for him, and she'll become twice as emotional. And the man will begin carrying a double load of responsibility for the aspects of life that require a more rational way of dealing with the world. He'll become even more detached emotionally. Both people can begin to break this impasse by taking a step to develop their opposite sides.

*

*I am
developing and integrating my
opposite polarities.*

*

My relationships express
aspects of myself

Think of a person in your life whom you are having a problem with. It could be your mate, somebody at work, one of your children, someone else in your family; it could be a friend. Ask yourself what qualities that person has that are very different from yours. How does that person express something that's really different from the way you express yourself? That person may be reflecting some aspect of you that you don't know about or allow yourself. If that quality seems negative to you, look to find some underlying positive essence.

For example, if he or she is pushy and aggressive, perhaps a part of you that needs to be more assertive is being mirrored. If he or she seems lazy, maybe a more relaxed aspect of you is being reflected.

*

I'm discovering
the mirror in each of my
relationships.

*

What are you judgmental about?

It can be difficult for us to recognize or accept that people we have problems with are actually mirroring for us the disowned parts of ourselves. One simple way to tell is when you feel very judgmental toward that person. Underneath, you may be jealous. Perhaps this person is expressing a kind of energy that you hold back or don't allow yourself to express. They may be out of balance in an opposite way from you. It's not necessary to become like they are, or go to an extreme. Just recognize that you may need to allow yourself to develop a little more of that energy.

For example, if you are a quiet, reserved person you might feel judgmental toward someone who seems to grab a lot of attention. They may be mirroring a part of you who'd like to receive more attention.

*

Where in my life am I
being judgmental, toward myself or others?
How is that showing me a part of myself
that I don't accept?

*

Avoidance and acceptance

We avoid the things that we're afraid of because we think there will be dire consequences if we confront them. But the truly dire consequences in our lives come from avoiding things that we need to learn about or discover. We must instead learn to accept the things we're afraid of, whether it's exploring our emotions, or learning to balance our checkbook! Acceptance is simply a willingness to look at, confront, and understand something instead of pushing it away.

Acceptance doesn't mean that we have to allow things into our lives that aren't good for us. We need to set boundaries and be able to discriminate between what's right and not right for us.

*

I am
willing to confront and understand
all aspects of myself and
of life.

*

Take external action first

Being willing to learn from our relationships does not mean that we should stay in relationships that are not good for us. If a relationship is physically or emotionally abusive, what we have to learn from it is how to set boundaries and protect ourselves. This means leaving the relationship if that is the way to take care of ourselves effectively.

People can criticize or abuse us only to the degree that we accept or allow it. First we must take steps externally to take care of ourselves. Then we must look inside to heal the way that we criticize or abuse ourselves, and begin to love and support ourselves instead.

*

I *set*
appropriate boundaries to protect
and take care of
myself.

*

Acknowledge positive mirrors

When we first begin to look at our relationships as mirrors, we have a tendency to see only the negative. It's important to acknowledge the positive feedback you're getting from your relationships as well as the negative. Take the time to note what's positive and beautiful about what you've created in your life, because that is also a reflection of who you are. Use what you see that's negative, not as a reason to beat yourself up, but as what you have yet to learn to improve this masterpiece that you're working on. Your life is an ongoing work in progress; you're always improving and defining it.

*

Through
the positive reflections of my life,
I see how beautiful
I am.

*

Role models mirror my own
inner qualities

Think about someone who has qualities that you admire. What is it that you appreciate about this person? Do you feel that you have those same qualities? You may not yet be in touch with them, or you may not have yet developed them to the same degree as this person, but they are there. Pretend right now that you have a part of you that's very much like this person, and think about how you can activate and express that part more in your life. Think about how this person would act in a given situation and allow his or her energy to come through you. And ask your own inner guide to show you more about how you can bring forth those qualities in yourself.

*

The qualities I see
in my role model are already in me.
Each day I am learning to express
that part of myself.

*

We will always need relationships

Sometimes people wonder if we're going to need relationships anymore once we've become integrated and whole. Since relationships seem to be teaching us the ways in which we are not yet complete, once we learn these lessons it seems relationships might become superfluous. But of course there is no final outcome, there is no point at which we will be "done." There is just an ongoing, ever-deepening process of discovery.

Part of our humanness is to need love, contact, interaction, and closeness with other people. The more conscious we become, the more our relationships reflect our many facets. Our relationships will be enhanced only as we express more of who we are.

*

My relationships
are an important part of
my life.

*

Our relationships can be healed

For many of us, our relationships have been such a painful struggle that it's difficult to believe we could get to a place in our lives when all relationships are primarily supportive and satisfying. Yet, if we are willing to do our deep emotional work, our relationships will mirror every step of progress that we make in our relationship with ourselves. As we become more integrated, our relationships become an incredible reflection of our aliveness, self-love, and self-expression.

*

My relationships
are getting better and better as I am
healing myself.

*

The mirroring dance

A conscious relationship is a dance where you are continuously seeing yourself mirrored through the other person. You constantly reflect each other's process. As you move into one polarity you see the other person moving into the other. You play together and enhance each other. Sometimes you get stuck for a while. You challenge each other to greater expression of all that you are. It's an ongoing, deepening, opening process. You are dancing with each other and with life.

*

I am
dancing through life with those
I love.

*

Sex is energy

Our sexuality is related to the flow of energy, the life force within us. It can't be separated from what's happening energetically in the relationship. It's intimately connected with how we're dealing with our emotions and how clear we are feeling. The more we've experienced and expressed our feelings, the clearer our channels are and the more freely and pleasurably the sexual energy can flow.

*

*My sexual
energy is flowing freely and
clearly.*

*

Sexuality requires honesty

One of the key things in a sexual relationship is honesty. How real and authentic are you being? How much are you truly expressing what you feel? Are you withholding anything? These are harder questions to answer than we may think, because there are so many levels of honesty and dishonesty, both with ourselves and with others.

On one level, we may consciously choose not to talk about things that we're feeling or doing because we don't think it's going to be accepted by the other person. On another level, we may not even allow ourselves to know what we really feel because we're afraid it will be unacceptable to the other person, it will upset things, it will make that person angry. We subtly withhold information or feelings without even being aware of it. Ultimately, it's because we fear that we'll be rejected or abandoned by the other person.

*

I
express my feelings
honestly.

*

Dishonesty deadens relationships

Any time we begin to withhold our truth on any level, no matter how small or subtle, we begin to block the life force coming through us and we begin to deaden ourselves and our relationship. The sexual energy, among everything else, diminishes. That is what often happens in long-term relationships.

It's very difficult to stay truly honest with ourselves and with each other in every moment. It's the nature of human beings to try to please the other person, which means we don't want to show them the parts of ourselves that are undesirable. We also want security, so we are afraid to risk revealing something that could threaten the relationship. There's a subtle level at which we withhold truth. To whatever degree we withold truths, there is a corresponding level of energy dying in the relationship.

*

The more truthful
I can be, the more alive
I feel.

*

Risk honesty

It's possible to have an alive, passionate, self-renewing relationship that remains sexual, or at least that continues to go through very sexual cycles.

Ironically, you have to be willing to risk the relationship in order to have the relationship stay alive. You have to face your fear of losing the relationship in order to be authentic, to be yourself, and to live your truth. You have to be willing to show the parts of yourself you want to hide because you feel they are undesirable and could threaten the relationship. And if you *are* willing to do that, you could lose the relationship, but more likely you will create a very alive, powerful relationship.

*

I
risk being
real.

*

Sexuality goes in cycles

There are times in our lives when we feel sexual, and others when we don't. Our relationships also do and don't feel sexual at times. We have to acknowledge that and respect these cycles. Sometimes when we're not feeling that energy, we may fear that it is permanently lost! But like everything else in nature, there is a rhythm to our sexual cycles. At certain times we need to turn inward and nourish ourselves with alone time. This replenishes our energy so that once again we feel the desire to merge with another.

*

*I respect
my natural energy
cycles.*

*

Sex exists on many levels

Sex exists on all four levels—spiritual, mental, emotional, and physical. Sex on the spiritual level involves the profound connection that we can feel to another being, the tantric connection of merging with another soul. The mental level of sexuality is fantasy, connecting to all the possibilities that exist through our minds. The emotional level of sexuality brings the satisfaction of love and closeness. The physical level of sexuality provides release and fulfillment for our bodies. Any one of these levels can be satisfying, but to feel complete we need to experience them all.

*

I *am*
opening all levels of my
sexuality.

*

The drug crisis

The drug epidemic in our society is related to the cultural imbalance of our masculine and feminine polarities. Our overemphasis on the male energy, the need to produce and to drive ourselves, has suppressed our female energies—our creative, intuitive, and spiritual connection. Some drugs reinforce that tendency—allowing us to feel powerful and in control. Other drugs take us out of the linear left-brain into the right-brain, visionary, spiritual, and intuitive creative energy. Of course they do it in a very distorted and destructive way. But they allow us to spend time on the other side of our psyches.

If we want to heal the drug crisis, we need to find healthy, creative ways to support people in exploring and balancing both polarities.

*

I am
finding healthy ways to express
both my masculine and feminine
energies.

*

We all have addictions

We live in an addictive society and we almost all have a tendency toward some type of addictive behavior. We may be addictive with food or drugs (including cigarettes, coffee, and sugar), we may have addictive patterns with money or relationships, or we may be workaholics. Even meditation is an addiction for many people. Any behavior that we compulsively use as an escape from our feelings, or a substitute for satisfying our real emotional needs can become an addiction. Our culture has not taught us effective ways to fulfill our needs and lead a balanced life, so we must discover this for ourselves.

*

*I am learning
to fulfill my needs in natural,
balanced ways.*

*

Drugs inhibit the primary
selves

Alcohol and certain other drugs inhibit the primary selves. They inhibit the inner critic temporarily. They knock the pusher out, they knock the protector/controller out, and they allow the disowned selves to come forward. The more emotional selves, the more spontaneous, expressive, sexual, sensuous energy—all of those selves that don't get a chance to come out otherwise come forth.

And then, of course, once the drug wears off, once the alcohol wears off, the primary selves come back heavier than ever, particularly the inner critic. This perpetuates the cycle. Because when you wake up the morning after and your critic is killing you, you want to knock it out again as fast as possible. Once you stop this negative cycle, you can become aware of the inner process and do the consciousness work to bring yourself into balance.

*

I am learning
healthy ways to let my disowned selves
find expression.

*

Tyrant and rebel

Many people with addiction problems are heavily identified with the rebel aspect of their personalities. They are caught in the inner tyrant/rebel conflict. The inner tyrant has many rules about what we should and shouldn't do, and it's the rebel's job to do the exact opposite of what the rules say. Being dominated by your inner rebel is not true freedom—it's an unconscious, knee-jerk reaction that can be very destructive. Freedom is attained through consciousness—becoming aware of your inner tyrant *and* inner rebel and no longer being controlled by either of them. Ironically, both are trying in their own way to take care of you, but it's not working. It's time to stop being controlled by either of them.

*

Do I *have*
tyrant and rebel aspects to
my personality?

*

Addiction equals need for love

The child in us has certain basic needs—for love, emotional and physical contact, respect, and self-expression. If these needs weren't fully met in childhood (as they seldom were), we develop certain behaviors to try to nurture our inner child. Our addictive patterns are actually unconscious and misguided attempts to care for our child. Through overeating, drinking alcohol, smoking, or taking drugs, we try to nourish the child, numb its pain, and make it feel better for a little while; or through overworking ourselves or caretaking others we try to gain validation from others and a feeling of security.

Of course it doesn't work very well because it's not taking care of the child's real needs and it's terribly destructive to our bodies and psyches. What works is to stop the addictive behavior so we can get in touch with what the child really needs, then take steps to begin providing it.

*

Am I using
any addictive ways to nurture
my inner child?

*

Reach out for support

One of the most important steps in dealing with any type of addiction is to reach out for help and support from others who truly understand. It's a communication to yourself that you are worth supporting and caring for. Many people have found effective support for dealing with their addictions through Alcoholics Anonymous, Al-Anon, and other twelve-step programs. These programs provide group support, acceptance, and nurturing, which many people didn't get in their families and don't have in their lives any other way. They also foster an atmosphere of unconditional acceptance, which is the opposite of the inner critic.

Since most people with addiction problems have strong inner critics, in going to meetings they start to counteract the effects of that inner self-criticism, and learn more about unconditional love for themselves.

*

I am finding
the kind of love and support I need
in my life.

*

We need a spiritual connection

One of the reasons why the twelve-step programs are so effective is because they are helping people find direct spiritual connections so they don't have to use drugs to have those same feelings or effects. The programs provide a place for people to find their own experience of their higher power, which is one of the main things people are looking for with drugs.

Once we get emotional support from other people and begin to make contact with our inner spiritual essence, we have the basic foundation to do our psychological healing work.

*

I am
in touch with my
higher power.

*

What is your relationship
to food?

Food is one of the major things we use to substitute for love, for power, for protection in this life. It serves a lot of functions. If your inner child is not being nurtured and loved, then one thing you may unconsciously do is try to give it love through giving it certain types of food. But the real thing that's needed is love, emotional contact, and/or allowing yourself to feel and express your emotions.

*

I give
my inner child real love,
not substitutes.

*

Sugar is a substitute for love

Many people use sugar as a substitute for love. It gives you the same kind of high you get when you feel loved. Chocolate has a particularly powerful effect. Sugar is the drug for the inner child that gives the child that temporary sensation of bliss. As an occasional treat it's fine, but it's not a substitute for the love the child needs. What are some other, healthier ways that you can give your inner child a special treat and make it feel happy and loved?

*

I'm finding
healthy ways to "treat" my
inner child.

*

Caffeine is a drug

Caffeine is a drug that reinforces the emphasis on the masculine values of productivity and rationality. Most people have a cup of coffee in the morning to "get going." They literally jump-start their bodies so they can get to work and produce. But when you artificially stimulate your body you put yourself out of touch with your natural rhythms. You become out of touch with your body, and so out of touch with your emotions.

To let go of caffeine, you have to be willing to find your body's own natural speed and rhythm, and trust that.

*

I *am*
learning to trust my body's
own rhythms.

*

Food can be a substitute
for male energy

Food and weight issues are related to distortions and imbalances in our masculine and feminine energy. If you have a developed female energy and less developed male energy, you may feel somewhat unsafe and ungrounded in the world. Food becomes a substitute for male energy—a way of protecting the vulnerable child and grounding yourself through excess weight on the physical body. Or, you may feel a sense of power and control in your life through denying yourself food. One way to heal these issues is to begin developing a constructive inner male energy to support and ground you.

*

I am allowing
my masculine energy to support me
in the world.

*

Learn to set boundaries

Food and weight issues have to do with boundaries. If you don't know how to set clear boundaries by being able to say no to people, or how to protect yourself and keep people out of your space if you need to and want to, you may literally create a protection physically through excess weight on your body. The extra weight provides a sense of solidity, strength, and groundedness, and the extra "padding" actually keeps you from absorbing as many energies from around you. It's the body's attempt to protect the vulnerable child who's very sensitive and picks up on everybody's feelings and emotions and energies.

When you don't feel like you know how to give yourself protection, you'll eat both to nourish the child and to create a layer of protection around it so that you can feel safer and function in the world.

*

I protect
my vulnerable child by setting
clear boundaries.

*

Food is not your mother

Food issues often revolve in some way around mother, or the nurturing, mothering energy. We need to learn to nurture and mother ourselves, instead of still acting out what we did or didn't get from our own mothers.

You can become a good mother to your inner child by nourishing the child with love and understanding and support. And you can be the good father to your inner child by giving the child protection and structure to support it. Whether you're a man or a woman, you have to cultivate the good mother and the good father energies within yourself toward your own child.

*

I *am*
a good mother and father
to my inner child.

*

Balance nutrition and enjoyment

We tend to give ourselves an awful lot of rules and regulations about what we should eat and shouldn't eat. We try to follow different diets and different ideas of what's good for us; then we rebel against them. Being a good parent to your inner child means feeding yourself food that is both nutritious and enjoyable. Find a balance of food that is healthy and wholesome, but that also tastes good and is what your child enjoys.

*

I *eat*
delicious, nutritious
food.

*

*Find out what your body
likes to eat*

Your body naturally tells you what you want to eat
when you're not using the food as a substitute for
something else. Then you can actually start listening to your body and finding out what your body
likes and doesn't like. The body is very clear. If you
eat what your body wants most of the time instead
of what you think it should eat, your body will
respond by feeling healthy, happy, and alive. You
will find that what your body wants is what is truly
good for it.

*

*Today I am
taking the time to notice
how my body responds to what
I eat.*

*

The practice of conscious eating

The practice of conscious eating involves three steps of awareness. First, deal with the emotional issues: why you eat, what you eat, and what you're really trying to accomplish. Find out the deeper level of what the inner child needs, and learn to nurture and protect the child in more effective ways than with food. Second, begin to learn to communicate with your body to find out what your body really wants, when it wants it, and what it enjoys. And know that that changes from time to time, according to where you're living, what the weather's like, what your energy is like, what you are doing, and what kind of life-style you have. The third step is how you actually eat: Where do you eat, how do you prepare your food, how much time do you give yourself to eat?

*

I *am*
becoming conscious about
eating.

*

Take time to eat

How much time do you give yourself to eat your meals? Do you sit down? Do you allow yourself to experience the moment, enjoying the taste of each bite? Or do you eat a quick sandwich at your desk while you are working?

We need to take time to nourish ourselves each day, to feed and love and care for our inner child.

*

Today
I give myself plenty of time
to eat.

*

Create a space for yourself
when you eat

Where do you eat, physically? Do you create an attractive space for yourself? Do you give yourself enough room? Do you sit down?

We need to give ourselves the room to enjoy and digest our food, so that it can nourish us. We need to love ourselves enough to make the meal and the space beautiful.

*

Today I create
a pleasant space for myself
when I eat.

*

Prepare your food with love

No matter what you are eating today, it is important that it be prepared with love. Don't just throw it together. You deserve better than that. Think about the food while you are preparing it and appreciate it for the way it looks, the way it smells, and the way you anticipate how it will taste. Create an intention to nourish yourself lovingly with this food. Take an extra minute or two to arrange it attractively on a beautiful plate, and set the table for yourself even if you are eating alone.

*

Today
I prepare my food with
love.

*

Feed yourself on many levels

Food is a compact form of energy, and it feeds us energetically at the same time it feeds us physically. But we have other levels besides our physical bodies that are being nourished when we eat. The emotional level can also be fed while we're eating by thinking about nourishing our inner child with this food and nourishing ourselves emotionally with things that look, smell, and taste good.

Let eating be a pleasurable, self-loving experience. You are feeding yourself on spiritual or etheric levels, too. Think about where this food comes from in the earth and how the earth is nourishing you. You can get nourishment on all these levels if you tune into them while you eat.

*

*I nourish
myself on many
levels.*

*

Excitement

Excitement in its natural form is what we experience when we feel the life force moving through us. It's a state of high attunement, with lots of life energy flowing through our bodies. But what many of us are experiencing as excitement in our lives is actually a form of adrenaline addiction. We get addicted to creating a lot of drama or intense struggle in our lives that gives us a drug high from the adrenaline in our system.

The difference between an addictive type of excitement and a natural excitement is that the former really isn't fulfilling and satisfying in the long run. It drains us and exhausts us. True excitement enlivens us, because it emerges from following the natural flow of our energy.

*

I *feel*
the natural excitement of
being alive.

*

The connection between excitement
and fear

Excitement and fear are closely connected. Often, we experience excitement as fear before we allow ourselves to open to the excitement. A classic example of this is stage fright. The amount of life force that's about to move through us in performance is very exhilarating and powerful. It's almost as if the body is frightened of the amount of energy that's going to come through it, so the initial experience is to tighten up against it, which we feel as fear. But what's really underneath it is aliveness and excitement.

*

Sometimes,
when I feel afraid,
I may also be
excited.

*

Male and female sides
of sexuality

To fully experience sexuality, we have to be able to access both the male and the female sides of it. Traditionally, men own the male side of their sexuality, but disown the female side. So men are comfortable being aggressive, making a conquest, and being physical. Women carry the more sensuous and emotional aspects of sex, so they experience the more sensitive and vulnerable aspects of their sexuality.

Of course, these generalizations are often reversed. Some men have developed their sensitivity and sensuality, but are uncomfortable with the aggressive aspect of their sexuality. And some women enjoy their physical sexuality, but fear true emotional vulnerability. As with anything else, if we are stuck in expressing only one polarity, we are missing the other half of life. If we develop both polarities of our sexuality, we can enjoy moving back and forth freely to experience all our energies.

*

I enjoy expressing
the male and female sides of
my sexuality.

*

Polarities create sexuality

The essence of sexuality is the magnetism that exists between two opposite energies of the universe. The greatest charge, aliveness, and energy there is is the polarity between the male and female energies. Whether a relationship is heterosexual or homosexual, we are attracted toward qualities in the other person that are opposite from our own primary characteristics. As we use the reflection from our partner to help us embrace those opposite qualities within ourselves, we develop the full range of our own expression.

*

What energies
attract me most
strongly?

*

Discover your animal self

As civilized human beings, we have all disowned a part of ourselves—our animal selves. This is the part of us that's physical and instinctual, that knows how to survive and flourish in the physical realm. It includes our physical bodies, our instincts, our sexuality, and the natural aggression that allows us to protect and take care of ourselves.

We have become very frightened and distrustful of these aspects of ourselves, because they are opposite of our mental and spiritual energies. Yet, this is a part of ourselves that we need. By disowning our animal selves, we have lost touch with a great deal of our power and our ability to thrive in the physical world. We need to get back in touch with our animal selves and draw from their powerful energies.

*

*I am learning
to recognize the animal aspect
of myself.*

*

Our natural sexuality
has been disowned

Because we have disowned our primal animal selves, most of us have lost our natural connection to our physical sexuality. In fact, many people feel a great deal of shame and inner conflict about their sexual feelings and their bodies. Ironically, when we deny or disown something, we often become obsessed by the very thing we're trying so hard not to think about! So our culture has become quite obsessed with physical sexuality—as we see in our movies, magazines, music, and many other aspects of popular culture. This is because our physical sexuality is an important aspect of our being that we're longing to reconnect with. If we can accept and own that energy, it can become a natural, integrated part of our lives.

*

My sexuality
is a natural part of
my life.

*

*

Own your own aggression

When you disown something in yourself one of the things you do is project it onto other people. Then it becomes your shadow, and you blame the other people for it. Yet, by disowning and projecting it, you give it power.

Many people these days are very identified with peace, love, and spirituality. They disown their aggression and project it on those other people out there who are making war. Then they meditate and pray for peace. They don't realize that by disowning their aggression they are creating a huge shadow side that's actually empowering war! To *really* create peace in the world, we must make peace with our natural aggression and learn to use it appropriately.

*

I *am learning*
to recognize and accept my
aggressive energy.

*

The warrior

To own your own aggression, you must recognize and honor the part of yourself that is the warrior. The warrior is a very important part of both men and women. The warrior is the part of us that's strong, aggressive, and protective. It's the part that will set limits and take action if those limits are challenged. Its function is to preserve our safety and well-being, and to serve truth and right.

*

I honor
the warrior within
me.

*

The warrior protects us

If you don't have access to your warrior, which is really the part of you that can protect and take care of you physically and energetically in the world, you are a victim and can be hurt or abused.

If you've disowned your warrior, you are not protected. It's as if there's a hole in your energy field and you draw in violence and abusive energy. So it's vital to connect to and have access to that warrior energy for your own protection.

The Eastern martial arts cultivate access to your warrior energy to such an extent that you never need to use it. Your energy field contains that powerful energy, and that alone protects you.

*

My inner warrior
is a powerful energy
that is always guarding and protecting
me.

*

Channel your warrior

In our culture we have lost an appropriate place for the warrior energy to be expressed and honored.

The old role of the warrior is dying. For many of us, it's no longer appropriate to go out and physically fight and kill others. There's no real place for that warrior energy in the way there used to be, and yet it's an essential archetype. It's important that we find the right use and expression of that energy. Otherwise, it will find a negative outlet or turn inward.

Each man and woman needs to connect with his or her own inner warrior and find a way to channel it. Our warrior is the energy that protects so that we can walk through potential danger unharmed. It's the part that can help us stand up for what we need, want, or believe in. We must become warriors for truth, who take the path of confronting life, cutting through denial, and living in truth and integrity.

*

I *am*
a warrior for truth and
life.

*

How not to create war

Two things create war. One is to identify with the warrior unconsciously, so that you think that aggression is the only way to handle things. That way overtly creates war. The second, which supports the first way, is to disown aggression, project it onto other people, and end up creating war because you've disowned it in yourself.

The only way to truly create peace in the world is to not be identified with either of those sides, and to really own and recognize both the peace lover in yourself and the warrior.

*

*I honor
my peace lover and my
warrior.*

*

The inner child is the source
of creativity

It's important to get in touch with our inner child because the child is the key to our creativity. Very young children are endlessly creative because they have not yet become inhibited. They play with their imagination easily. They love to draw and paint. They sing little songs. They dance. They're magically creative beings.

All of us are that way, too. We all had that magical, creative essence within us as children. As adults we have suppressed it. As we get in touch with the child inside us, we release our creativity.

*

My
creative inner child is coming
out to play.

*

*The key to creativity is being
willing to risk*

The key to creativity is being willing to try something, to risk doing it and see what happens. Our creative inner child is the part of us that's not afraid to try new things. When children draw pictures, they don't worry about whether the pictures are going to look exactly the way some critic thinks they should look. They do it for the joy of it. That's how our creative energy can be fed, by feeling the essence of that child within us and being willing to try things that are fun, enjoyable, exciting, new, and different. As we get in touch with our inner child, we open whole new areas of creativity within ourselves, which is immensely fun and rewarding.

*

*As I am willing
to risk doing new things,
I find the source of my
creativity.*

*

We are all creative beings

Many people think they're not creative. This idea comes from some early conditioning we've received. Somebody along the way told us we weren't creative, and we believed it. Or maybe we got so much criticism or disapproval that we were afraid to try anymore. In one way or another, we did not receive enough encouragement and support to express our natural creativity, so we came to the conclusion that we weren't creative. But, after we break through our limiting ideas, blocks, and fears, we are all creative beings.

*

*I
am a creative
being.*

*

There are many ways to
be creative

Many people tend to equate creativity with only certain types of expression. We all know that art or dance or music is creative, for example, but we don't necessarily think that running a business or running a home or being a parent is also creative. And yet, these are all highly creative activities. In fact, raising children can be a tremendously creative contribution to the world.

In order to appreciate how creative you are, start to think about the things you do that are enjoyable, that come naturally and easily to you. Can you see the creative aspects of these things? Can you appreciate how they express an important aspect of your being?

*

I *recognize*
the creativity in all the things
I *do.*

*

To be creative, you must risk

To be creative, it is essential to take some risks. It helps to try small things first. Do just one new and different thing. Fantasize about a creative thing you would like to do. See if there is some small step you can take in the direction of that fantasy.

Many people have the concept that they're too old to try something new, that if they didn't start when they were children it's too late now. It's never too late. Remember, you never have to show anyone what you do. You are doing it for yourself, to give yourself freedom and joy.

*

Today
I will risk doing one new,
creative thing.

*

Our bodies are a form
of creative expression

We know that each of us is in essence a creative being, a spiritual being who comes into a physical form. That physical form is our first act of creation. As we change internally, our bodies, as the expression of our spirit, change also. The more you come to know, acknowledge, and express your creative spirit, the more your spirit shows in your primary creative project—your body.

Observe the ways you block yourself from expressing your spirit, and see how that is reflected in your body. As you remove these blocks to your creative expression, your body will reflect that transformation.

*

My body
is an expression of my creative
spirit.

*

The inner critic can block creativity

As adults, the major block to our creativity is our inner critic, that part of us that internally criticizes what we do. Our inner critic has standards of perfection incorporated from the world around us, ways that it thinks things *should* be done. The critic's job is to criticize us when we are not doing things the way it feels they should be done. For most of us, this inner critic is what stops us from taking the kinds of risks that need to be taken to be creative.

Those of us who have allowed our creativity to flow in our lives have managed in one way or another to set our critic aside long enough to let the energy come through spontaneously.

*

*I let
my creative energy flow in
my life.*

*

The perfectionist can hamper creativity

If you have a heavy perfectionist, it's difficult to create because nothing is ever going to be remotely good enough for it. You need to develop an opposite voice—one that encourages you to try things without worrying too much about results. It can be helpful to have a "creativity support system"—a person or people in your life who give you encouragement to try your creative ideas, without judgment. As Maxwell Perkins said, "Just get it down on paper, and then we'll see what to do with it."

*

My creative
expressions don't have to be
perfect.

*

Find a new direction

Many people are creative in one area of their lives, but not in other areas. If you have one area in which you're creative, you have an advantage in that you know what it's like to allow that creative channel to flow. Think about whatever it is you do in that aspect of your life. If you play music or you're creative in business, what is it that allows you to be creative? How do you get your inner critic out of the way? How do you trust yourself and express yourself?

Think about how you can take the same method you use in your creative area and apply it in other areas of your life, how you can apply it with something new or different so that you allow your creativity to flow in a new direction.

*

*I'm expressing
my creativity in new areas
of my life.*

*

Creativity requires experimentation

The fundamental principle of creativity is that you express *something*. You have to let the expressions flow. You must be willing to allow things to be expressed that are not perfect or wonderful. People who are creative are willing to make mistakes. Almost all successful people say that they have had more failures than they've had successes. They have tried many things that have not always worked for them. Some have been very disappointing, but they have continued to take risks and try again.

*

I am willing
to make mistakes and learn
from them.

*

Lighten up!

Creativity requires play. It requires fun. It requires a sense of adventure. Learn to look at things a little more lightly and not take them so seriously. If we take ourselves too seriously, we can't have that adventurousness that allows us to explore in new places.

*

*I approach
this day with a sense
of adventure.*

*

Creative clearing process

Here's a suggestion for clearing some blocks and starting your creative energy flowing. Get several large pieces of paper and some beautiful colored pens. Find a quiet, private place. Tune into whatever feelings you have inside that say you aren't creative. Take a colored pen and write down all the doubting, self-critical thoughts and feelings. Then tune into your inner creative voice. Take a different colored pen and a different paper and write down all the feelings, ideas, and fantasies of your creative voice. On a third piece of paper, using any colors you want, draw a picture of yourself (literal or abstract) expressing your creativity in the world. Don't worry about whether your picture is artistic. Just let your creative child come out to play.

*

My
creative inner child is having
fun.

*

Creativity creates joy
and spontaneity

The purpose of cultivating our creativity is our own enjoyment. It's to feel the feeling of being a channel, allowing the creative force to come through us. If we keep that focus in everything we do, we will begin to de-emphasize the necessity for doing things perfectly or producing an exact result. We will begin to get the same kind of pleasure out of life that children do when they are spontaneously moving with their energy and doing what they feel.

*

I *let*
the creative energy flow
through me.

*

Fantasize

We all have fantasies about what we would do if only we could. Give yourself a chance to fantasize freely. Enjoy it! Ask yourself: What kinds of things do I love doing? What comes easily to me? What's fun? What do I do so naturally that I don't even think about it? How could I expand it? Could I possibly make a living from doing the things I find most enjoyable and the most fun? Try not to limit yourself. Be open to all kinds of possibilities that you've never allowed yourself to imagine before. Today, explore and express your fantasies in your mind, in writing, in drawing, in talking with someone else.

*

I *am*
enjoying my creative
fantasies.

*

Try something different

Look for little ways to express yourself more creatively and differently. Don't aim too high and get discouraged. Start with small things. Let yourself take a step that's fun and relatively easy and enjoyable. Then appreciate yourself for that. If you keep taking small steps, you will end up being exactly where you need to be. Have fun with it.

What it really boils down to is this: You can do things in the same old way you've always done them, which is safe and secure, but also a bit dull and boring, or you can try something new and different. The reason we don't try new things is because our protector selves are afraid they are not safe for us. But if we reassure those parts of ourselves, and don't try to do too many new things at once, we can create more excitement and fun in our lives.

*

*Today
I will try something
different.*

*

Creativity equals masculine
plus feminine

Creativity is a blend of masculine and feminine energies. It's the receiving of that creative force (feminine) and the expression of it (masculine). The way we normally think of the word "creative," as in a creative type of person, is the more feminine, spontaneous, less-structured, "artistic" type. But actually, creativity is the ability to manifest creative spirit in the physical world. It's really an integration of the two principles. Having creative ability and not manifesting it is not being creative. And producing without connection to the source is not creativity, either. True creativity requires both free-flowing inspiration and focused discipline.

*

I manifest
my creativity through inspiration
and discipline.

*

Connect to your female energy

Find a quiet place, either indoors or outdoors, where there is enough space to move around and where no one will disturb you. Stand in a comfortable position with your knees slightly bent. Breathe slowly and deeply. Imagine the nurturing, female energy of the earth coming up through the soles of your feet and filling your whole body. Begin walking or moving around, feeling the female energy in your body. Allow yourself to feel open, sensuous, receptive, intuitive, powerful. Sense your connection with everything around you. If you are a woman, imagine that you are a goddess. If you are a man, imagine that you have a goddess within you. Move your body with the energy of that goddess.

*

I allow
female energy to flow
through me.

*

Connect to your male energy

Find a quiet place, either indoors or outdoors, where there is enough space to move around and where no one will disturb you. Stand in a comfortable position with your knees slightly bent. Breathe slowly and deeply. Imagine that you are taking in male energy through every cell of your body. Let yourself be filled with this male energy. Begin walking or moving around with this energy. Allow yourself to feel strong, clear, focused, powerful. Sense your individuality, your distinctiveness from everything around you. If you are a man, imagine that you are a god. If you are a woman, imagine that you have a god within you. Move your body with the energy of that god.

*

I *allow*
male energy to flow
through me.

*

Balance your male and
female energies

Notice the difference in how your body feels when your female energy is running through you and when your male energy is running through you. Be aware of how differently you relate to your environment from each perspective. Each is important, each is powerful. Play with these different energies in your life, let them come through you when you need them. Experiment with bringing both of them in at the same time to see if you can experience a balance of the two.

*

I'm finding
the balance of my male
and female energies
in my life.

*

The creative process is cyclical

The creative process is cyclical. It's a moving back and forth between the male and female energies. It doesn't mean that you should try to be perfectly balanced at all times. Usually you will be in one place for a while and then move into the next. It's important to have a balance. As you become more aware of what the different energies feel like, you will be able to tell what mode you're working in. The trick is to learn how to recognize when you've been in one mode too long, and allow the shift to happen.

*

I am
becoming aware of my own shifts
between masculine and feminine
modes.

*

Excess male energy

Male energy, once it gets going, tends not to want to stop. After a while, you're running on empty. If it feels like you're putting out more than you're taking in, or you're pushing or forcing or getting burned out or tired, that's a message that you've gone past the place when you needed to stop and go into the more female mode. Oftentimes it takes the form of your not knowing what to do. The male energy gets frantic, because all it knows is *doing*. It will want to keep doing things, even though it's not appropriate. If you push past this point, you may go into a depressed state or become sick. In some way, you will be forced into more balance.

*

*I am
learning to recognize
my male energy.*

*

Excess female energy

When we have been too long in the female mode, we have a problem producing. We may have many very creative ideas, but they stay in the planning stages, they don't take physical form. The female energy might fear the compromises that are necessary when an idea takes physical form. In our fantasies, our ideas are always perfect. When we have to put them on paper, we must face the fact that we could fail. Choosing to stay with the perfection of fantasy is being too much in the female mode.

*

I *am*
learning to recognize my
female energy.

*

A time of exploration

In the traditional male and female roles, men have been totally identified with their male energy and women have been completely identified with their female energy. We were all stuck in rigid roles, expressing only half our potential and disowning the opposite polarity. Men have suffered as much as women from cutting off one side of their psyches. While women felt disempowered in the world, men have been disconnected from feelings and intimacy, which is extremely painful. Fortunately, we live in a time when we are finally free to explore and express all aspects of who we are.

*

*I'm exploring
and expressing all aspects
of myself.*

*

The challenge of our times

When it comes to male and female roles, we live in a challenging but confusing time. Now we are free to explore our opposite polarities, but we are having difficulty finding the balance. Many women have developed their masculine energies, and many men have been cultivating their feminine aspects. Now many of us feel somewhat stuck in these new polarities. Now women are wondering how they can be powerful and successful in the world and still have emotional and sexual intimacy, home, and family. And men are trying to figure out how to be sensitive, vulnerable, and able to express their feelings while still owning their power and aggressive energy.

*

*I'm finding
a balance of my male and female
energies.*

*

Integrating male and female: women

Women have played the traditional feminine role of staying home with the family and being the nurturers for so long that a lot of women nowadays have gone to the opposite extreme. They have gone out there in that very male world, have become businesswomen, very driven and very career oriented. They've put very little attention on home and family and relationships—all those traditional roles.

But that is an extreme, and so now many women are realizing that they want the balance. They want satisfaction and fulfillment in both career and home life. It's a challenging goal and one that is necessary and possible to achieve.

*

I'm finding
satisfaction in my work and my
relationships.

*

Integrating male and female: men

Many men are feeling extremely lost in this time of changing roles. Men are faced with quite a dilemma: how to be sensitive and develop their female sides without losing their masculine sides. It's bewildering right now. They don't know how to support themselves emotionally, and I don't think most women know how to support them very well, either. A lot of men nowadays have gone into that feminine side of sensitivity, intuition, vulnerability, and emotion. But there are no role models of how to keep that side without losing the masculine side. We need to be sensitive to how great a challenge this is.

*

I

am sensitive and
powerful.

*

The new man

What is maleness? What is it to be a man—an integrated, male/female being—in a male body? Men have few role models for what the new male is all about. The men who are doing this kind of work and facing themselves really *are* the new role models. It's their own inner intuitive sense of knowing that will tell them what they have to do. They can't look to the women in their lives to teach them. They have to look to their own inner sense of truth and to each other. Men have to give each other a lot of emotional support.

Women are always so busy trying to figure out what they have to do to help men. It's not up to women. It's up to women to work on themselves.

*

Men: I *am*
becoming an integrated man.
Women: I *respect and appreciate*
the men in my life.

*

The new woman

What is femaleness? What is it to be a woman—an integrated, female/male being—in a female body? The job for women is to let go of that subtle way that even liberated, New Age women unconsciously have of focusing on trying to get the men squared away, trying to fix them or make them right. We need to communicate directly and honestly with the men in our lives about what we want and don't want, like and don't like, and how we feel. Then we need to look into ourselves, to take care of our integration of our own male and female selves. This is very difficult, because we really like to focus on the men.

*

Women: I *focus*
on my own process.
Men: I *respect and appreciate*
the women in my life.

*

Enthusiasm

Enthusiasm is a quality that arises naturally from the flow of the life force within us, carrying us toward new experiences and discoveries. For many, this quality was squelched in childhood when we were not allowed or encouraged to follow our spontaneous creative impulses. We can begin to cultivate our enthusiasm by trusting and following our intuitive feelings, exploring new experiences, and doing the things that we truly love to do.

*

I am
enthusiastic about
my life.

*

Life shows us what we need
to know

Follow creative ideas and creative impulses. Do what is in your heart. As long as you follow that, you will be guided as to what you need to do next. When you live your life this way, allowing yourself to be guided, it doesn't mean that you don't make mistakes or have failures. It does mean that fundamentally, your life can work much more powerfully. But you must be willing to let things go when they're not working, and keep going with what is working.

*

I trust
the process of moving with my own
creativity.

*

Life is a learning process

To make your life work, you have to become aware of what isn't working. When you are willing to do your own spiritual and psychological process, you will keep learning and growing from your experiences. Use the feedback from your life when things aren't working, rather than just being a victim. Recognize that when things aren't working externally, it's a reflection of something that's not working on the inside. Some piece is missing or something needs to be recognized.

I've been committed to using my life this way. That has enabled me to take the stuck places and make them into learning experiences. When I take the next step of my own growth, simultaneously things start to work on the physical plane. Do the work. Then things will start to shift.

*

I *use*
the feedback I get from my life
to change and grow.

*

True wealth is simple
and balanced

For many people, financial wealth and physical possessions are addictions. We're trying to fulfill ourselves with things, instead of what we really want and need that we don't have, such as love, emotional contact, and creative self-expression. The more conscious and integrated we become, the more our lives reflect that with intimacy, love, creative satisfaction, and fulfillment, and the less we are driven to accumulate money and possessions.

As we move with the flow of our natural energy, our lives fall into simplicity and balance. We have everything our hearts could desire in great abundance, but we don't accumulate excess. We're not wasting; we're not using resources that really don't need to be used.

*

I *give myself*
the things I really need
and live in simplicity
and abundance.

*

Money is a mirror

Your relationship with money can be looked at in the same way as you look at other relationships— as a very powerful reflection of your own process of integrating all the energies within yourself. Money reflects your relationship with your creative energy.

Money really isn't anything in itself. It's symbolic. Money represents creative energy. The way money flows in your life has something to do with the way your own life energy flows. How you handle this energy will be reflected in how money works for you.

*

How is money
working in my life? What might it
be mirroring about how my energy
is flowing?

*

The male energy
approach to money

The male energy approach to money is focused on the physical, on getting the job done in the world. That tends to produce money. Men and women with strong male energy usually are able to bring in money and handle it in practical ways. But their underlying feeling is that they are doing it by their own effort. They often feel disconnected from the power of the universe, so there is a lot of work and struggle, and oftentimes eventual burnout and exhaustion. They also lose intimacy, joy, playfulness, and pleasure in life.

If you are overly identified with male energy, money isn't about enjoying—it's about hard work and making a living and being responsible.

*

Am I overly serious
and driven in relationship
to money?

*

*The female energy
approach to money*

Men and women who are more identified with their feminine polarity are often creative, artistic, and spontaneous. They may have a tendency to be impractical with money and little desire to deal with the details. They don't want to balance their checkbooks or make budgets because it feels like such details will limit them and suppress their free spirits. They tend to spend too much and then get into trouble financially. They may have the philosophy that the universe will handle it all, which is a spiritual truth, but if you are out of balance, such a philosophy can lead to financial struggle. Often, this type of person will have difficulty putting energy into the world in a way that's effective—the classic stuggling artist.

*

*Do I have
a tendency to be impractical
with money?*

*

The money conflict

The two opposite polarities of male and female energy are often mirrored in conflicts about money in a relationship. One partner may be careful, practical, and very responsible with money. The other partner may be much more playful and free-spending. This conflict can cause painful problems unless both partners can recognize that each one mirrors what the other needs to develop, and begin to do the work to cultivate that opposite polarity.

*

Do I have conflict
with anyone over money matters?
What is it mirroring
to me?

*

*What makes you need
to control money?*

If you tend to be too driven or too controlling about money, ask yourself what would happen if you relaxed about money. What if you allowed it to flow? For the more masculine kind of money personality, the fear is that relaxing will make you vulnerable. It's easy to go out and do in the world, but the receiving function is blocked. To receive means to open up to vulnerability. It also means getting in touch with a lighter kind of approach, easing up a little, not taking things so seriously. You don't have to carry the burden of such heavy responsibility. If you learn to trust and relax more, the universe can take care of you.

*

*I'm learning
to relax and trust that I will be
taken care of.*

*

What frightens you about money?

If you have difficulty handling money responsibly, ask yourself what it is that frightens you about handling money. What part of you is frightened? What self in you are you disowning? For the more childlike, spontaneous, creative personality, there is often a fear of growing up, because growing up means losing your magic. Handling the daily details of life, including financial details, in a responsible, adult way may feel as if it will stifle your creative spirit.

But form (money) and spirit (creativity) do not have to be enemies. Understand that the function of form is to support spirit in the physical world and make it possible for spirit to live comfortably and positively in the physical world. Learning to manage money realistically and wisely will actually support your creative spirit in being expressed more effectively in the world.

*

Managing my money
responsibly supports my creativity
and freedom.

*

Accept your responsibility for money

When it comes to money, don't function as a child wanting somebody else to be the responsible parent. If you don't hold the energy of responsibility for your own money, it doesn't matter how much you have or are able to bring into your life. Someone will take advantage of you and you'll lose it, or you'll create some kind of disaster. You have to take responsibility for your money and learn enough so that you can make intelligent decisions. Activate your inner "financial manager," and be open to learning whatever you need to know from others who understand how to manage money wisely.

*

I am learning
to manage my money
wisely and well.

*

*Needing money may be
a guiding force*

Sometimes we do things only because we need the money. This can seem like a negative motivation, but it may be the universe at work. That motivation can force us out into the world to learn something or to do creative work that we might not otherwise have done. If you need money, that may be the universe directing you to do a certain thing for your own growth. Getting money for it is the universe's way of telling you that you're doing the right thing. As long as you're following your guidance and doing what you're told, you will benefit from the experience.

*

*Has the need
for money ever guided me
into an important learning
experience?*

*

We work toward
a fulfilling career

At times, it can be appropriate to have a job that's just about paying bills. It may be giving you stability you need at this time, and the skills you are learning may be useful later. If you find yourself drawn toward work that doesn't seem as if it will ultimately be right for you, you probably need either the skills or some experience that will give you something of value toward your really meaningful work in life.

*

Everything I am doing
is contributing to the truly meaningful
work that is my purpose in life.

*

Money does not really
belong to us

Money is symbolic of the flow of life energy that comes from the infinite source. The more you are trusting and following your own energy, the better money will work in your life. It will come into its proper balance.

I've learned to listen to what I feel is the higher force and do what it tells me to do. And then it provides me the money to do it.

*

As I listen
to my higher guidance, money flows
into my life.

*

True success

What is true success? Is true success just having a fabulously successful business and making a lot of money? Or is success leading a balanced, integrated life in which we find fulfillment and happiness? One part of success is accomplishing something, giving something to the world and receiving validation, appreciation, and money as a result. But our society's male model of doing business does not leave space for those other things— like a fulfilling family life or good health.

*

I define
success in my own way,
according to what gives me fulfillment
and happiness.

*

Every job contributes to the whole

There's a basic human need to feel that we are serving and making a contribution to the world in some way. As our society has gotten more complex, many of us have lost the sense of how what we do connects to and is of service to the rest of the world. That leads to a feeling of dissatisfaction and emptiness—an emotional bankruptcy. No matter what your work is, you *are* performing a vital service. Take a look at what it is you do and try to see how you are making a contribution. See the direct link between your work and others. It is only then that you can feel fulfilled and satisfied by your work.

*

*Through my work
I am contributing to
the world.*

*

*Work does not have to be
a struggle*

We tend to have a belief system that says work involves sacrifice and deprivation. We have to struggle and work hard for survival; expecting it to be totally fulfilling is not realistic. We need to release this old idea. We have a right to have work that's meaningful. We must create a new belief system that says life is meant to be fulfilling, that our work is meant to be exciting and a really passionate part of life. We can expect that and create it.

*

*My work is
a passionate and fulfilling part
of my life.*

*

Be an employee of the universe

Truly serving the higher good turns out to be doing exactly what you most love. Sharing your passion in life and doing the things that really excite you is your soul's expression into the physical world. It will always be the greatest service you can do. Life becomes a wonderful circle where you are doing what you love, and it also serves others. The satisfaction of serving the universe is your greatest reward.

*

I'm serving
my higher power. I'm doing what
it tells me to do.

*

*Your higher power
provides everything*

Once you've made the decision to serve your higher power, it becomes your higher power's job to provide you with everything you need to do the work it wants you to do. My higher power always provides me with just the right person I need to do a certain thing or to give me the correct advice. Money is provided so that I can continue to do my job. As long as I keep asking for and receiving guidance on what I'm here to do, I receive everything I need to do it.

*

I *am*
learning to trust
that my higher power will provide
what I *need.*

*

Time for what's important

We can gain satisfaction in our work only to the degree that we also have other satisfying things in our lives. Part of creating a successful work life is to also consider some of the other categories of things that are important in our lives, such as time alone, intimate time with loved ones, time for physical activities, play time, and entertainment. Making a daily, weekly, or monthly schedule that includes all of these elements can help to ensure that you create time for all the things you want in life. It's a sign of self-worth to give yourself the time you need for all that is important to you.

*

*Am I allowing time
in my life for everything that's truly important
to me?*

*

Create structure to support yourself

If left to our own devices, most of us in modern society don't just naturally create a life-style that includes all the elements that we need. We have to consciously create structure in both time and money to support our balance and integration. This means consciously considering what we need to include, and then setting up some kind of time schedule and budget that supports us in including those things. It won't just happen. We have to create it.

*

How can I begin
to create a time schedule and a budget
that's realistic and includes
the elements I need?

*

Structured time

Time needs to be structured within the workday as well, because work has different elements to it. For example, your job could include time focused on business matters, time dealing with other people, time being creative, and time doing paperwork. It can help greatly to work out a schedule within your work time so that you have a certain part of the day doing work alone at your desk and part of the day communicating with others, in the way that works best for you.

*

I *structure*
my workday in a way that
supports balance.

*

Creative motivation comes
from inside and out

Creation of anything, whether it's a painting, music, a new product, or an annual report, comes essentially from two forces: inner inspiration and external need. Sometimes the inner motivation comes first, but sometimes external pressures move you into a creative process that you may not have come to from inside.

The creative process is an interplay between that inner creative impulse and practical realities that come from the outside. If we do things only from outer motivation, we lose our inspiration and start creating things that have little depth or value. If we go too far in that direction, we lose our creative source. On the other hand, we can't just produce in a vacuum without some motivation from the outside. We have to balance the two. Oftentimes an external factor becomes a catalyst to move the creative process that has gotten stuck on the inside.

*

My creativity
is stimulated by internal and
external factors.

*

Inner conflict

We all have a considerable amount of inner conflict at times in our lives. Inner conflict arises from the various parts of our personalities needing and wanting different things. Instead of thinking that we have to resolve the conflict by choosing one or the other option and eliminating the rest, we must try to expand our awareness to include new possibilities.

The trick is to become conscious of all the different needs, feelings, and forces going on inside and to expand to contain them all, without knowing how that conflict will be resolved. Be willing to hold all the polarities of your inner conflict in your consciousness without immediately trying to solve it. Then, from that place of consciousness and awareness, a solution and an integration actually come from a higher part of your being.

*

I am aware
of all sides of the conflict
inside me.

*

Substitute "and" for "or"

The painful thing about conflict is that we think we have to sacrifice one part of what we want or need in order to get the other. It's very difficult with our logical, left-brain minds to see how there could be any other choice. We're so used to thinking in a linear fashion that we think if we want this then we can't have that. But we can have both. It's not something that happens instantly, but if we're willing to have patience and go through our process, the universe will give us the essence of everything that we need.

*

*I can have
everything I really need and
want in life.*

*

Be in conflict consciously

If you are in a state of conflict, allow yourself to be there consciously for a while. Be as aware as possible of all the different conflicting feelings and parts of you. Embrace it all. Then ask for the higher creative intelligence within you to find a way of resolving and integrating all the important aspects of yourself, rather than having to choose one or the other. Don't expect an instant solution. Allow time for your process to work itself through organically. Your inner guidance will bring you awareness of your next step.

*

I am consciously
allowing time for my inner conflicts
to resolve themselves
organically.

*

Going to extremes

There are times in the process of finding balance and integration when it's appropriate to go to an extreme, especially if it's an opposite extreme from one you've already explored or developed. There's nothing wrong if that's what your inner guidance tells you you need and that's what feels good and right for you at the time. Sooner or later, life will move you out of any extreme into a balanced flow between both polarities. Once you are comfortable anywhere on a given spectrum, you're free to move through the full range of experience.

*

*I'm free
to explore the full spectrum
of life experiences.*

*

Be conscious of your polarities

The more you are in touch with the opposite polarities within your own personality, the more conscious you are. When you start to go a little too far in one direction, you'll feel the other part of you pull you back into balance. And then if you start going too far in that direction, the first polarity will pull you back again. You will feel increasing balance, flow, and integration within yourself, and it will be mirrored in all aspects of your life.

*

*I'm conscious
of the many opposite energies
within me.*

*

Look for the lesson

The universe tells you what you need to focus on. It gives you little nudges. If you've learned to recognize those signals, then you quickly catch whatever in your life is not in balance. But most of us don't know how to recognize the little nudges the universe gives us, so then we get a stronger poke. Eventually, we get slapped across the face or knocked down. And some people have to really hit bottom before they are willing to look at the necessity of change and the possibility of growth.

Try to cultivate the attitude that the problems that come in your life really are gifts from your own soul trying to call your attention to the things in your life that are not in balance. Then life is less traumatic. You can immediately look at a problem and ask, "What do I need to learn here?"

*

What is the universe
trying to tell me? Today I will be open
to receiving its message.

*

*Outer conflict is a mirror
of inner conflict*

Most of our conflicts in relationships or in situations in our lives are projections of inner conflicts. People we are in conflict with are usually mirroring some parts of ourselves with which we are uncomfortable or unresolved.

For example, people who are always getting into trouble with authority figures haven't owned and accepted the authoritarian parts of themselves. People who are very identified with a structured, authoritarian voice will probably attract into their lives rebellious people—particularly their children.

This situation won't change until we're willing to see the outer conflicts as mirroring our inner conflicts. As we become aware of and accept all aspects of ourselves, outer conflicts melt away.

*

*I am
learning to see outer conflict
as a mirror of my own inner
conflict.*

*

World conflict is a mirror
of inner conflict

National or international conflict is a mass projection of every individual's internal conflict and the internal conflicts that may exist inside of that particular society. We project parts of those conflicts onto other people, other cultures, and other races, and then we go out and start wars and conflicts with them. It's all mirroring the conflicts inside ourselves. If we look at the opposing sides of international conflicts, we can see what each country or culture is rejecting in its own society. World conflicts won't end until each society accepts and allows all the different archetypal energies to find expression.

*

How might
current world conflicts mirror
my own inner conflicts?

*

*The polarities of developed
and undeveloped countries*

The Third World countries are all cultures that are rooted more in the feminine principle than are developed countries. They have a greater connection to the earth, to intuition, to spirit. But they are not as developed technologically. They don't have the male aspect that would allow them to get out there and make their way in the world. They suffer as a result. They are overrun and taken advantage of by the male energy-dominated cultures. We industrialized nations suffer, too, from our lack of connection to the earth. Each side has to learn from the other. We all need balance. The world needs balance.

*

*As I find balance
within myself I help the world
become more balanced.*

*

Imagine balance and harmony

Get in a comfortable position. Relax, close your eyes, and take a few slow, deep breaths. Move your awareness into a deep, quiet place inside. Begin to imagine what your life would be like if it were truly in balance and harmony. Once you have a sense of that possibility, begin to expand it to imagine the people around you, your community, and your country all finding balance with one another and the earth. Finally, imagine the entire world living in balance and harmony.

*

*The world
is coming into balance
and harmony.*

*

Fall

We need relationships

Our primary relationship is with ourselves, and ultimately that's the only one that can provide the foundation for wholeness. That's the place where we need to find integration and balance. And at the same time, we need relationships with other people in order to be happy and fulfilled in life. If we only look for wholeness and completion within ourselves, we disown the part of ourselves that also needs other people.

Human beings are social creatures. Physically, emotionally, mentally, and spiritually—we absolutely need close contact with other people. We need love, support, understanding, recognition, and stimulation reflected to us by others.

*

I spend time
cultivating my relationship with myself
and time reaching out to receive
what I need from others.

*

The inner child is a key
to intimacy

Because the inner child is the part of us that feels the deepest emotions, it's the part of us that can truly love. It's also the part of us that's vulnerable, the part that can be wounded or hurt. To feel real intimacy with another person we must be in touch with our vulnerability, with our love, even with our ability to be wounded.

If we are not in touch with our inner child, we will not experience true intimacy. As we learn to be in touch with the child, to take care of and protect the child, and to express the child in appropriate ways, we can experience intimacy in healthy, fulfilling ways in our lives.

*

As I learn
to support my inner child
I experience greater intimacy
in my life.

*

We all have needs

As human beings, we need a lot from other people.
We need love, support, connection, and closeness.
In our society, feelings of dependency are considered negative. We're supposed to be very self-
sufficient. It's shameful to most people to admit
how much they really do need, especially emotionally. But our needs are what make us human.
We have to learn to honor them, not deny them.
Then we can begin to get our needs met.

*

*It's natural
for me to have emotional
needs.*

*

Express your needs directly

If you recognize and admit your needs, and really honor them, you can then express them directly. Only then can you begin to receive from other people. If I can say I really need your love, I really need your friendship, I really need a hug right now, or I need someone to talk to, it's usually pretty easy for people to give. But if I say, "I shouldn't need anybody," then my needs will come out in indirect ways and take on greater energy, because I'm denying what is really there. Then it becomes hard for people to respond without feeling manipulated or overwhelmed.

*

*I'm learning
to ask for what I need clearly
and directly.*

*

We are all vulnerable

Most of us are somewhat afraid of our vulnerability. We have various ways of masking it, hiding it, defending it. The key to intimacy, though, is being able to be vulnerable with another person. To do that, we must first be honest with ourselves about our deepest, most vulnerable feelings. We must learn to care for and protect these feelings, not by closing them off and defending them, but by being able to say honestly what we feel and ask for what we need.

As we learn to use our inner strength to support and express our inner vulnerability instead of to repress it, we begin to feel safer and more comfortable opening up to another person.

*

*I am learning
to feel comfortable with
my vulnerability.*

*

Ambivalence toward relationships

Many people, especially women, say they really want committed relationships and can't understand why they're not happening. Many of us have a hard time recognizing how much inner conflict and ambivalence we really have about committed relationships. We may have one strong voice that wants intimacy and closeness, but there is another, hidden part that's really frightened of commitment because, for most of us, close relationships have meant some sort of loss of self. We may be unaware that parts of us are working against having a relationship. In fact, we usually project that feeling outward and find only unavailable partners!

The first step toward creating a close relationship is to recognize and honor the part of us that *doesn't* want it, and find out why it feels that way.

*

What part of me
doesn't want close relationships,
and why?

*

Polarities in relationships

The feminine side of our being is looking for merging and closeness. The male side is looking for individuality, independence, freedom of movement, and self-expression. The male side of us fears being tied down, restricted, limited, or swallowed up by the feminine. The female side fears separation and abandonment by the male. If we're more identified with our male energy in relationships, we'll feel independent, but we'll attract partners who mirror our disowned yearning for closeness. If we're more in touch with our female energy in relationships, we'll feel strong desire for more intimacy, but attract partners who want more space!

*

Which polarity do I
identify most with at this time?
Am I in touch with the other side
of my feelings?

*

Space in relationships

In an intimate relationship we need both closeness and space. We need to merge with another, and also we need to keep coming back to our own individual sense of self. Being sensitive to our own needs and being able to take space when we need it is difficult. We tend to lose that ability when we merge with someone else. But if we don't take space when we need it, we will create a conflict or problem that will allow us to separate.

It's challenging, but it's essential that we learn to take space more consciously. Once we've had a certain amount of closeness we need to separate and have some time and space to ourselves, which may be anything from a few minutes to a few days. Intimate relationship is a constant dance between the polarities of closeness and space.

*

I *can*
consciously take space
when I *need it.*

*

The inner child may fear relationships

The child inside us may prevent us from entering into an intimate relationship because it is frightened. At its core, the child yearns for closeness and intimacy more than anything else. But if the child has been wounded by earlier relationships in our lives, it may be terrified about being smothered, abused, rejected, or abandoned again. If we become consciously aware of the fears of our inner child, we can give it the love and support it needs to feel safe in moving into relationships.

*

*As I grow
more conscious of my inner child's fears,
I am able to care
for its needs.*

*

Be truthful in relationships

The difficulties in our relationships and in our lives come when we are withholding our truth because we are afraid someone won't like it or in some way there will be dire consequences. The minute you start hiding the truth, you have a problem in the relationship. You begin to subtly withhold yourself from the relationship, and then the relationship will suffer in aliveness.

An intimate relationship, or any relationship that's important, needs to be based on truth and realness or it will die. To whatever degree you're not truthful in a relationship is the degree to which the relationship suffers.

*

*Am I aware
of any ways that I withhold my truth
in relationships?*

*

We create distance in relationships

It may feel incredibly scary to be truly honest in a close relationship. Because if you let someone get close enough to really see you as you are and you lose that someone, you may feel devastated. Yet, if you keep that person too far away, then you won't get enough of what you need. So we keep people at arm's length, close enough to have some contact, but not close enough to really see us. We fear that if they find out who we are they might not want to be with us. Therefore, we try to have just that degree of intimacy, but no more. Unfortunately, keeping this distance leaves us unsatisfied in our relationships.

To find the fulfillment of intimacy, we have to take the risk to let others see us as we really are.

*

I'm willing
to share myself as
I really am.

*

Honesty requires courage

It takes a lot of courage to be honest in a relationship. On the one hand we need to be real and authentic with another person, and on the other hand we're afraid that it may lead to abandonment. It's important to understand and respect that conflict within yourself. You can't expect yourself to go out and start telling the absolute truth to everyone every minute. That would be very frightening. You just try to work your way in that direction, understanding that it is very scary for part of you, and at the same time that if you don't express your truth you will sacrifice part of yourself in the relationship. Gradually, you will learn to start being more authentic.

*

What part of me
is afraid to be truthful and why?
Can I understand and respect that part
while learning to be more open?

*

Stay true to yourself

Every time we don't tell the truth we abandon ourselves, because we're not allowing ourselves to feel. We are saying to the child in us, "I can't let you come out. I can't be real, I can't show who you really are." We essentially abandon ourselves to be with the other person, and that feels terrible.

When you do start making the choice to stay true to yourself and risk losing the other person, you strengthen that bond with yourself. Ironically, the more you honor your own relationship with yourself, the better your other relationships will be.

*

*I'm learning
to stay with myself even when
it's scary.*

*

Be truthful with yourself

Being honest doesn't mean you have to say exactly what you are feeling every minute or report every thought that passes through your mind. It's not even appropriate to reveal yourself to everyone. First and foremost, being honest means being truthful with yourself. Then you can consciously choose whether or not you will share that with someone else. The more intimacy and depth you desire to have in a relationship, the more you will share. If you are not sure exactly what you are feeling at any given moment, just share what you are in touch with and allow the clarity to emerge gradually.

*

I am
honest with myself
and others.

*

Act in accordance
with the truth

If we get in the habit of listening to the truth inside ourselves every day, then we can begin to live in accordance with it. We can speak the truth as we feel it. We can act on the truth as we feel it. We can live our own truth.

*

Today,
I am acting according to
my own truth.

*

Honest communication

To be most effective in communicating with someone, you have to be willing to tell the person about your own feelings, not just your judgments about him or her. Then the other person will be more likely to hear you. For example, "It really hurt my feelings when I was talking and you interrupted me. Sometimes I feel like you aren't really listening to me and that really hurts. I feel like I'm not important." That's very different from saying, "You know what, you are self-centered! You never listen to anybody else and I think it's time you dealt with that."

If you're able to keep giving somebody your response from your own experience and be vulnerable enough to express your own feelings, then it's easier for the other person to listen without becoming defensive.

*

I *am*
learning to express my feelings
honestly.

*

Vulnerability attracts caring

One of the keys to successful relationships is learning to express your feeling from a vulnerable place instead of from a defensive or attacking place.

That's very difficult to do because when you're feeling vulnerable your every instinct is to defend and attack. At those times, even the people you love most in the world suddenly look like potential enemies and you want to defend yourself from them. But the more invulnerable you are, the less receptive somebody else will be. And the more you are able to share from the deepest part of yourself about what you're experiencing, the more likely it is that people will be touched and moved by it. They'll be able to hear it, because you're not pointing a finger at them or expecting something from them. Vulnerability draws people in and attracts compassion and support.

*

I am able
to show my vulnerability
with those I trust.

*

Communication versus criticism

Where do you draw the line between honest feed-back and destructive criticism? Unless somebody asks for feedback, don't automatically give it. If you have feedback for somebody, it's good to ask first if that person would like to hear it or not. And really provide a chance to say yes or no.

And on the other side, if somebody wants to give you feedback and you get a sense that you're about to be attacked, say no.

*

I *do not tolerate*
destructive criticism. I have the right
to say no or
to leave.

*

How to recognize abuse

A lot of us are so used to hearing abuse, both from others and from our own inner critic, that we don't even recognize it. Because it sounds familiar, we think we deserve it. Don't leave your inner child open to being beaten up. Start noticing your feelings. If you start feeling guilty and bad about yourself while somebody is talking to you, then take a look at how that person is talking to you. Is he or she sharing an experience and talking about its effect, or is that person pointing out what's wrong with you?

Any time somebody points out what's wrong with you or makes you wrong, that person's own vulnerability is being covered by attacking you. We all do that at times. But we can also learn to be conscious of when we're doing that to each other and learn to move into a deeper place to say what we're really feeling.

*

I *am*
learning to recognize
abuse.

*

Learn appropriate self-protection

If you have a pattern of attracting criticism or verbal abuse from others, you must learn appropriate self-protection. It's not appropriate to allow anyone to attack or abuse you verbally, emotionally, or physically. If someone is harshly criticizing you, say, "This doesn't feel good to me. Don't talk to me like that." If it doesn't stop, physically leave the room or the premises. Let the person know that you're willing to hear about feelings of hurt and anger if expressed in a nonabusive way, but that you're not willing to be criticized or attacked. We must learn to protect our inner child that way.

*

I am able
to set boundaries and limits
to protect myself.

*

Constructive criticism

We tend to look at everything with a critical eye and notice the things that are wrong about it, whether it's ourselves, or something that we do or create, or what other people do. A very strong, discriminating quality is important. But in looking at what *doesn't* work, don't overlook the things that *do* work. Consciously remind yourself to pay attention to the positive things and acknowledge yourself and other people for the things that are being done well.

*

I *recognize*
and appreciate the positive aspects
of every situation.

*

Criticism can cripple you

Many teachers use criticism in teaching. They think the way to help students learn is by being very stern and critical with them. But it usually makes the students' inner child feel really bad. Then they don't want to learn, and they don't want to expose themselves. In order to learn you have to put yourself in a very vulnerable position by admitting what you don't know. If that vulnerability has been wounded, the child will close itself off. Many people's creativity, and their ability to learn, has been stifled by teachers who didn't know how to get information across without using the critical function. It's really not necessary to do it that way. As adults now, we can reconnect with that child inside of us who was discouraged and help it to learn in a positive way by making it feel safe and loved and encouraged.

*

I am
supporting and encouraging
my inner child.

*

Take care of your own needs

There is a tendency in our society, especially among women, to sacrifice for others. Instead of taking care of our own needs, we give and give and give to other people, particularly our children. When we do this, there's an unconscious bill at the end. It says, "I took care of you, now you owe me. Now take care of me." Our children may then carry the burden of that guilt for the rest of their lives.

So it's important, particularly as parents, to take care of your own needs. If you can take care of yourself reasonably well as you go along, you can then set others free to live their own lives and take care of themselves. You show your child how to live life in a responsible way by taking care of yourself instead of expecting other people to do so for you. It's never too late to free your children by learning to take better care of your own needs.

*

Today I will
be conscious of what I need,
and I will take steps to meet
that need.

*

We all need time alone,
and time with others

We all need a minimum amount of time to be with ourselves each day. It's important to give ourselves that, no matter how many people there are who need us. (In fact, if you have many people who need you, you probably need alone time more than most!) It's a time when we can connect to who we really are and what we really need. It's a way to connect with our own inner knowingness.

As well as alone time we also need the feeling of closeness and connection to others. We need time alone with the person we are in relationship with. We need time with our friends. We need time with our children.

*

I recognize my need
for being alone and for being together.
I give myself both,
every day.

*

Allow yourself to receive

There's a part of all of us that is uncomfortable with receiving anything from anyone, because that would be admitting that we need something. That would leave us open to the worst possible outcome—being rejected. If you allow that fear to control you and you are not conscious of it, then you'll always be subconsciously asking for things, and yet not able to receive what anyone would give.

*

*Am I
afraid to
receive?*

*

Receiving is challenging

It's a greater challenge for many people in our culture to allow themselves to receive and feel good about receiving than it is to give. Receiving is difficult because it puts us in a vulnerable position. Giving is actually more popular because in giving we feel strong.

To be able to receive, you have to be in touch with your vulnerability and be comfortable with the part of you that needs. You have to be comfortable allowing another person to feel strong and powerful in your presence. Interestingly enough, the receiving position turns out to be extremely powerful in its capacity to empower others. If you want to make people feel good, let them give to you and then appreciate them for what they've given.

*

Today
I am practicing
receiving.

*

We don't have to be perfect with our children

As parents, we feel we always have to be in control. We feel we always have to be conscious, loving, and mature. Of course, it's not humanly possible. And it really isn't necessary.

The best gift you can give your children is to be real, authentic. Let them know that you too struggle with life, you too have emotions and feelings that are vulnerable. It doesn't mean you have to burden your children with your problems, but you can share with them your own real experiences. Tell them if you're having a hard day or feeling sad or angry, and let them know that it's not their fault. Share your moments of happiness with them, too. You can be honest with them.

*

Today I let go
a little of my need to be perfect.
I accept and share my authentic feelings.

*

There are few role models

There are few good role models for those of us who are on a path of consciousness. There may be a number of people who model various aspects of what we want, but there are very few individuals who model true integration. We may not find any one role model who has all the qualities that we want. We may need to draw inspiration from many people who mirror the different parts of ourselves that we want to develop. We must realize that we are role models for one another and for those who are coming along on the journey a step or two behind us.

*

I *draw*
inspiration from many people,
and I seek to inspire
many others.

*

Seek role models

If you know people who have the kinds of relationships you want or who relate to one another in ways
that you admire, let them be your role models. Let
them inspire your belief that you can have what
your heart desires in relationships. Be sure to look
beyond appearances, however, because relationships are rarely as good as they appear on the surface. But if you know people who have genuine love,
commitment, and communication, study them and
learn from them. Consciously visualize and affirm
that because this quality of relationship does exist
in the world, it is possible for you to have it, too.
Then be open to learning how to improve your own
relationships or creating the ones you want.

*

*It is possible
for me to have the kinds of relationships
I want.*

*

Bring the light into the dark

What a lot of people do, especially people who are on any kind of spiritual path, is divide the world into light and dark. We want to live in the light, and we don't want to go into the dark. We're trying to get out of the dark and into the light. But in fact, living in the light means bringing the light into every aspect of life—including the unconscious places that have been dark.

*

*I am bringing
the light of consciousness
into every aspect of myself
and my life.*

*

Explore your inner mansion

Imagine that you have a mansion. You live in several rooms, with the windows open and the light coming in, but there are some back rooms that you never go into. They're dark and closed off because you think something scary or bad is in there.

In the process of consciousness, as you have more power and courage and love for yourself, you begin to go one by one into those rooms and bring the light into them. And then you discover all the delightful places within yourself that you didn't know you had. Eventually you have the whole mansion. You can experience every room, and every room has its purpose. Without one of those rooms you don't experience all of who you are or all of what life is about.

*

*What rooms
in my inner house don't I go into?
Are there some that I could
explore now?*

*

Honor the journey

The process of consciousness is ongoing. It is a lifelong journey. It's not simply a matter of reading a book or doing a few affirmations, or using a certain process and your life is going to be all fixed. That's what many teachers promise. It sets up an unrealistic expectation. Especially on the emotional level, deep healing takes a certain number of years of focused work. Amazingly fast change *can* happen almost miraculously from any of these tools: creative visualization, learning to trust and follow your intuition, using voice dialogue. At the same time, it's an in-depth process. We go layer by layer, and we just keep learning, integrating, and opening more and more. There is no point at which it simply stops. There is no point at which we are "done."

*

I respect
the path I'm on.
I honor the lifelong journey
of consciousness.

*

Enlightenment occurs on four levels

Most people's process of enlightenment begins with having some form of spiritual experience, whether we recognize it as such or not. We have an opening to spirit and on some level we feel it or recognize it. Then we become curious about what it means and we begin to explore on the mental level of ideas. At some point we are confronted with the emotional level, which involves clearing the emotional blocks that we all have and healing the wounds that keep our life force from flowing through freely. Then we can bring the spirit fully into the physical body.

*

I am exploring
and integrating all four levels—
spiritual, mental, emotional,
and physical.

*

Depth of understanding

In the process of consciousness growth, there are many different levels of understanding. First, you learn a concept or a principle. Then you have to live with it for a while. Greater depth of understanding comes when you enact it in some small way. It is then that you become conscious of other levels. The important thing is to allow this process to happen. Don't be impatient to learn everything at once. And don't be angry with yourself when you discover how much you *didn't* understand before. Give yourself appreciation for all that you are learning day by day.

*

Day by day,
my depth of understanding
is increasing.

*

Let yourself feel

Our society has tremendous prohibitions against feeling too much. We are afraid to feel too much fear, hurt, sadness, or anger. On the flip side, we are also afraid to feel too much love, passion, or joy. We end up by expressing ourselves only in a narrow band of feelings and not going to any extremes. This prevents us from fully experiencing life.

*

I *am*
learning to feel all
my feelings.

*

Emotional healing

For many people, it's frightening to face healing the emotional level of their being. It's the level that people tend to resist the most. Exploring new ideas on a mental level is easy for us, because we're such a mental society. That's pretty safe. It doesn't shake us up too much. And many people are now following a spiritual path, hoping to become "enlightened" without having to face their shadow side.

But very few people know how to do true emotional healing. Even among therapists, healers, and workshop leaders, it's amazing how few people really understand how to guide others through their emotional healing process, because in order to guide others, they have to do their own! Yet, deep emotional healing is essential to becoming a conscious person.

*

I *am*
willing to do my emotional
healing.

*

How to begin to heal
the emotional level

To begin to heal on an emotional level, we have to risk looking at whatever is not working in our lives. There are trouble spots in our lives that are the universe's way of showing us what we need to work on. It could be any of a number of things: our physical health, weight issues, relationship problems, financial problems, addiction issues, or a problem child. And then we have to be willing to dig deeply and get in touch with the feelings that are connected to those trouble spots. We can't avoid those feelings. Once we're willing to receive the teaching in any life situation, our healing process can begin.

*

What is it that's not working
in my life? What is it I need to work on
to begin my emotional healing? I am
willing to risk looking at that.

*

Facing change and growth

Every one of us has a part that wants to change and grow. That part of us is willing to do whatever it takes to become conscious.

On the other hand, we all have a part that's afraid of change. This is a conservative aspect of our psyches that wants to protect us from unknown dangers. This part figures that because we've survived so far, it's safer to continue doing things exactly as we've been doing them rather than to risk real change.

Both of these aspects of self need to be respected. One of them inspires growth and carries us forward; the other one keeps us from moving too fast and becoming disoriented or overwhelmed. Sometimes it may feel like a tug of war inside. The trick is to honor both these parts and find a balanced pace of growth that they can both live with.

*

I'm growing
and changing at a pace that's comfortable
and exciting.

*

Fear of self-knowledge

Most people unconsciously choose to live in some degree of denial about their own thoughts and feelings. It can be frightening to begin looking inside and getting to really know yourself. The fear is that you are going to find out you are a defective person or in the depth of your being there is some dark secret.

One thing I can tell you for sure—there is nothing wrong with you. You are a beautiful, powerful being who may not have received enough love and support so that you could learn to really love yourself. In my own growth process and with thousands of people I've worked with, I've always found that facing the truth is healing and freeing. The deepest secret of all is that you are unique and perfect.

*

I am
willing to know myself
on all levels.

*

All wounds can be healed

In facing the fear of self-knowledge, it's important to know that all wounds can be healed. The emotional pain we all carry can be released through the process of looking deeply within, recognizing and acknowledging our thoughts, feelings and experiences, and allowing ourselves to feel and express our buried emotions.

To accomplish this kind of deep healing there are three necessary ingredients. First, you have to be willing to do the work, whatever it takes. Second, you have to get the right kind of support, whatever environment and people you need to assist and allow you to go through the process. Third, you need to allow the time that it takes to move through many layers of your psyche, usually a number of years. It's well worth it, though, to experience real freedom.

*

I'm giving myself
the commitment, support, and time
to become whole and free.

*

Our shadow

Our shadow is any part of ourselves, any energy within us, or any aspect of our being or personalities that we have not recognized, embraced, and expressed as a natural part of our daily lives. Like our shadow on a sunny day, it follows us wherever we go. It cannot be gotten rid of by ignoring it or by wishing it would go away. It is truly a part of us that desires our love and acceptance, that follows us around until we notice it and deal with it.

*

What parts of me
might be needing more acceptance and expression
in my life?

*

Meet your shadow

Your shadow is made up of whatever natural energies you have repressed or disowned. Energies that have been held down for a long time build up a lot of unexpressed power that can feel very frightening to confront. In essence, though, they are all natural and necessary energies that we need in order to live our lives successfully. To gain access to these energies we must find a way to begin getting acquainted with our shadow side.

*

*I'm willing
to become aware of
my shadow.*

*

Accept your shadow

Your shadow has been created by whatever has been sufficiently disapproved of by your family, community, or culture. Some people's shadow may be aggression, if their natural, healthy aggressive tendencies were repressed in childhood. They will need to learn to embrace their natural aggression—a quality of going after what they want in life. For others, the shadow might be vulnerability, if the expression of this quality was disapproved of in their families. They must learn to embrace their natural human needs and dependencies. For many people in our culture, our natural sensuality or sexuality has been pushed down and has become part of our shadow, individually and collectively. Embracing all these aspects of ourselves allows us to become healthy, whole, fulfilled human beings.

*

*I'm learning
to accept and embrace all aspects
of myself.*

*

The family shadow

You can often see how the shadow works within families. One child becomes the rebel or the scapegoat and begins to act out the disowned energies for everyone in the family. He or she is carrying the shadow for the entire family. That child begins to hate and blame him- or herself, and the rest of the family places blame, too, or focuses on trying to help. That way they don't have to face their own issues. When the scapegoat begins to go through a healing process and stops playing that role, the other members of the family are confronted with integrating their own shadow.

*

Am I,
or is anyone else in my family,
carrying the shadow
for others?

*

The collective shadow

You can see the collective shadow in operation whenever a social group or nation projects its disowned energies onto another race, ethnic group, or country and makes it into a feared and dreaded enemy. If you don't have an enemy, you don't have anybody to project your dark side on and you have to face it yourself. That can be painful and difficult. It's much easier to create a racial conflict or a cold or hot war.

To solve our personal and collective conflicts we must be willing to look within ourselves and own what we are projecting onto others.

*

As I accept
and integrate all aspects of myself,
I am healing the collective
shadow.

*

Visualization can't be used
for denial

Visualization is a powerful tool to create positive change in your life when used correctly. However, you can't use visualization to perpetuate your own denial of aspects of yourself. It won't work. You can't focus just on the positive or focus on the things that you like in life and that you are already comfortable with and can accept, and deny or try to get rid of the things that you don't like or don't want. That isn't the way the universe functions.

Life always confronts you with whatever it is you're hoping you don't have to deal with, until you can accept it. Visualization is meant to help you open to more of life, not close anything off.

*

Visualization
helps me open to all aspects
of myself and life.

*

Judgmentalness

Many people in the spiritual movement are trying hard to be nonjudgmental. We've recognized how our judgments separate us, and it's painful. In trying to be nonjudgmental, though, we're only cutting off the part of ourselves that *is* judgmental. We can't make it go away. It's a defensive reaction that has to do with something we're afraid of, something that we don't understand yet, or the times when we haven't expressed ourselves in some way.

Trying to be nonjudgmental is just a way of repressing a part of yourself. You are actually being judgmental of your judgmental self! Instead, recognize and accept the judgmental part of you, then look underneath it to see what's causing it to come forth.

*

I accept
my judgmental self
as a part of me.

*

Everything we do serves a purpose

The only reason we do anything is because it's the best way we've found so far to get our needs met, ensure our survival, bring us success, or make our lives feel worth living. Unfortunately, most of the unconscious ways we've found to fulfill our needs and take care of ourselves also have some very detrimental effects. That's why we need to replace our unconscious modes of self-nurturing and survival with conscious modes that are more positive and ultimately much more effective.

*

I am learning
conscious ways to take care
of myself.

*

Appreciate your old patterns

Appreciate all your patterns for what they have done for you. They were the best way that you could find until now, given your background and your experience in life, to survive and take care of yourself. It's important to appreciate all of them, no matter how negative they look, for what they've done for you. Start to take a look at what they have given you, what they have helped you with, what they've protected you from. Now you are outgrowing them, you are becoming more conscious of them, and they are starting to feel very limiting and uncomfortable. But as you begin to release them and allow them to transform into more appropriate ways of doing things, give thanks to them. They are like old friends who have gotten you this far in life.

*

I appreciate
my old patterns for getting me this far.
I'm ready to release and transform
those I no longer need.

*

You need what you need

Sometimes, it's difficult to admit that you needed your old patterns. You may feel critical of yourself for some of the ways you've coped with life in the past. But, if a child needs food to survive there's no point in saying to that child, "Well, you shouldn't need that food. You should learn to do without it." The child will find a way of getting the food or it will die. Well, the child inside us has certain needs for safety, nurturance, attention, and so on, that must be met. Our denial, our addictions, and all our other habit patterns are ways that we've unconsciously attempted to meet the needs of our inner child.

Now it's time to forgive ourselves for the ways we've tried to fulfill our needs in the past and to learn new ways that really work.

*

I forgive myself
for my old habits and patterns.
Now I'm learning positive, effective ways
to meet my needs.

*

There are always difficult times

In the journey of consciousness, there are inevitably times of difficulty and confusion. Often we make ourselves really wrong at those times. We beat ourselves up because we think we should already have it all together.

What we don't understand is that every time we move to a deeper level of understanding, there's a period of confusion. Often painful or scary emotions come up at those times. But each difficult time is rewarded by a real expansion and deepening of awareness. As we learn that this is a continuing process and stop expecting complete understanding at all times, it becomes easier and easier to get through those times of confusion.

*

*I am patient with myself
through the difficult times. I know that these, too,
will pass, and I will be rewarded
with greater understanding.*

*

Treat yourself like a friend

When you feel yourself starting to beat yourself up about something, there's a very simple technique that can help ease it. Pretend you are your best friend. How would you talk to your friend? You would never tell your best friend the things you tell yourself. You'd never treat anybody the way you treat yourself. You wouldn't talk to somebody you love that way, would you? Give yourself the compassion, friendship, and support you would to anyone you care about.

*

*I am
my own best
friend.*

*

Growth is cyclical

Growth is a cyclical process. Each time you go through a difficult stage you experience a dark night. Then you come into a morning and things feel good and easy for a while. You have the light of understanding. Then you face another challenge. This can occur on a daily, weekly, monthly, or yearly basis.

It's good to know that, at those times when you feel as if you don't know what you're doing, you are going through a cycle. It's part of the process.

*

I trust
the process of
growth.

*

Be confused

When you are going through a period of confusion, hang in there. Let yourself feel somewhat confused or disoriented or stuck. Sometimes you need to sit with these feelings for a while. It's okay to do that. Go inside and ask for guidance. Ask for what you're meant to be learning. Let yourself be guided to people or situations that can help you. Gradually, you'll move through it.

It's always worth it. Once you look back on a confusing period, you'll be able to see what you gained from it.

*

It's okay
to feel confused.
I am being guided to
what I need.

*

Stay with your process

When you are in confusion, it's not easy to stay with your process. Part of you wants one thing and part of you wants another. You want to decide once and for all, to come to a conclusion. But if you can hold all these different feelings in yourself and be aware of them—be in conflict, be in confusion, be in uncertainty—then the certainty will come from someplace deep within you. Your own inner truth will guide you. But if you try to cut this process short, you will deprive yourself of the opportunity to reach that place of certainty.

*

I am willing
to stay with my confusion
and conflict long enough to allow
a deeper truth to emerge.

*

Remember to trust

Each time you go through a cycle in the growth process, you gain a little more trust. But when you're in confusion, it's hard to remember anything. It's hard to remember that you've been through it before, and that the confusion is not a permanent state. On a deep level you may have that trust, but on another level you'll be saying, "God, why am I feeling like this? I don't understand what's happening." Consciously remind yourself that confusion happens. You will at some point have clarity. Understanding will come and you will receive a great gift from this experience.

*

I trust that there is
a gift in what I am experiencing.
Clarity and understanding will emerge
from this experience.

*

We need transition time

When we're going through big changes in our lives, we will often need a period when we don't do very much, whether it's a period of a few minutes, hours, days, months, or even sometimes a couple of years. It's a time of internal change and growth, and not a time for outward focus. When we are in that stage we often make ourselves wrong. "What's the matter with me? I'm not accomplishing anything. I don't even feel like getting out of bed in the morning."

If you are the kind of person who's been very productive and who's pushed yourself all your life, you may need to go through a stage of relaxing, being, letting things go, and just going through internal change. It's reassuring to tell yourself, "I've worked hard and done a lot in my life. Now it's time to rest and replenish myself."

*

I'm taking the time
I need to go through internal
transition.

*

The spiral journey

The journey of consciousness is really a spiral. We continually move through the same territory, but each time we move through it on a deeper level. Our patterns are basically there and we keep working through them and healing them on new levels. When you find the same lesson coming around again, don't think that you didn't learn it the first time. Know that you are a traveler on the spiral journey toward home.

*

*My journey
is a spiral. I appreciate each lesson
more deeply as I move
through new levels.*

*

There are three types of fear

There are three distinct experiences of fear. One is when there's actually danger and your intuition is a warning: "Don't go there. Don't do this. This isn't right." Respect that feeling completely and act on it. The second is when there's something that is not actually dangerous, but it's a challenge on the emotional level. Your inner child is frightened of it. Pause long enough to comfort the frightened child, see what's needed, and make sure that you are going to take care of yourself. Then, when your child feels ready, you can move into it. The third is when you know you're ready to do something, but it's definitely a challenge. The fear is a temporary reaction your body and psyche feel to the excitement of moving into a new level of aliveness. Recognize the fear as the flip side of excitement and ride it through.

*

I am learning
to respect and honor my fear.
Then I decide what action
to take.

*

Unconditional love

The higher intelligence of the universe loves us all unconditionally, and when we are in contact with that we experience a moment of unconditional love.

But human love is conditional. It's related to the needs and wants of our inner child. Trying to be unconditionally loving is an attempt to repress and deny your human self and be identified only with your spiritual self.

We need to allow our spiritual self to unconditionally love our human self, who is not unconditionally loving. We need first and foremost to learn to love our own experiences and our own process. Learn to accept your own personality for everything that it feels, including anger, hatred, selfishness, judgmentalness, and all the other things that you feel as part of the human experience. You can love other people only to the degree that you've come to love and accept yourself. That's just the way it is.

*

I *am*
learning to love myself
unconditionally.

*

Enlightenment of the form

The traditional concept of enlightenment involves opening to our connection with spirit and transcending the human form. That is not my idea of enlightenment. Reconnecting with the light of spirit is only the first step. The real challenge is to integrate our spiritual energy fully into our human form so that we can live in an enlightened way on the earth plane.

*

I *am*
on the path to
enlightenment.

*

What is your vision
of the future?

If we're honest, when we think about the future we feel hopeful and excited, as well as anxious, confused, and fearful. On a deep level we may even feel some despair.

We are living in a powerful time. It is both the most frightening and the most challenging time in human history. It is also the most exciting and the most hopeful time that has ever existed. It's no accident that we have all chosen to be here on the planet at this time. It's only by being aware of our feelings, both negative and positive, about the future that we can make the changes we want to make.

*

What is
my vision of
the future?

*

The world is in a healing crisis

It's only by going through a crisis in our lives that we begin to seek truth. We are going through that kind of crisis on a planetary level now. We are expanding in consciousness, and so the old forms that used to fit for us don't fit anymore. They are actually falling apart.

What's happening is that all those things that we couldn't deal with in the past are beginning to come to the surface. It can look very scary right now, because we are able to face the things that we couldn't see before. We have to become conscious of what doesn't work before we can become conscious of what to do about it.

*

I see
the healing process in my own life
and in the world.

*

Change often comes through crisis

It's usually when things in our lives begin to fall apart that we finally realize there's got to be a different way of doing things. We have to be shaken up. At first it's very frightening. It seems like a disaster, but it opens the door that allows us in to a deeper level of understanding, awareness, and growth. All of us find this process happening over and over again. As soon as we've healed ourselves on one level, something else will happen to take us to the next level.

*

*I'm willing
to learn from every
experience.*

*

*Things look their worst just before
they start to get better*

When things look their worst, it's comforting to realize that it's because you finally have something to contrast it with! You finally have an understanding or an experience that tells you that life *can* be better than this, that there is another way. And then the next step is to turn around and confront all those aspects that are not yet healed, that are not yet harmonious, that are not yet integrated and working in your life.

*

*I am healing
myself on deeper and deeper
levels.*

*

True healing

True healing comes from owning and accepting all of life's energies within ourselves. When we allow ourselves to begin to know the sides of ourselves we have disowned, we discover they are not as scary as we had imagined. When they are allowed to be expressed, they take their places as important facets of our nature. There is no split between "good" and "bad." All aspects of life are elements of the life force and facets of the divine.

*

*I accept
all sides of
myself.*

*

Commit yourself to the
healing process

In this world we live in four realms at once: the spiritual, mental, emotional, and physical. In order to truly heal ourselves and the world, we must heal all four levels and bring them into balance and integration. It's time for every one of us to make a commitment to our own healing and to the healing of our planet.

*

I *commit*
myself to the path
of healing.

*

Healing the spiritual level

Most of us in the modern world have experienced a profound disconnection from our spiritual selves and from the universal source. This causes an underlying feeling of emptiness and meaninglessness in our lives, which we seek to fill in many fruitless ways. Spiritual healing occurs as we begin to consciously reconnect with our spiritual essence and experience being filled by the spirit within.

*

*I am healing
the spiritual level
of my being.*

*

Healing the mental level

We all have many thoughts, ideas, and beliefs that, although they may have served us in the past, are now limiting our potential for expanding our consciousness. Mental healing occurs as we identify and gradually release belief systems that no longer serve us and explore new ideas that give support to a fuller expression of all we are. Also, some people have disowned their own intelligence through childhood experiences of criticism or other emotional trauma, so mental healing may involve reclaiming one's original intelligence.

*

*I am healing
the mental level
of my being.*

*

Healing the emotional level

To heal ourselves on the emotional level we must reconnect with and allow ourselves to feel and release our repressed emotions from the past. We can learn to accept and experience all our feelings spontaneously, fully, and freely. Emotional healing involves being in touch with our vulnerabilities, and learning to care for and protect them consciously and appropriately in relationships and in the world.

*

I am healing
the emotional level
of my being.

*

Healing the physical level

Modern civilized life does not generally encourage us to respect or be sensitive to our physical bodies. In fact, many of us are quite disconnected from our true physical needs. Physical healing takes place as we learn to feel and listen to our bodies again. Our bodies communicate clearly and specifically; as we learn to respond to our bodies' needs, we become attuned to our own natural rhythms and those of the earth.

*

I am healing
the physical level
of my being.

*

All levels affect each other

All four levels of being are closely related to and affect one another. As we heal one level we support the healing process on all other levels as well. Strengthening our spiritual connection gives us the inspiration and strength to face deep emotional healing, for example. As we do our emotional work, we release blocked energies on the mental and physical levels as well. And the more in tune we are with our physical bodies, the more energy we feel on every level. We may begin the process on any level and explore the various realms at different times in our lives. The ultimate goal is integration of them all.

*

*I am
integrating all levels
of my being.*

*

Growth is a lifelong process

There's a concept often held by people in the personal growth movement that it's all pretty simple—all you have to do is change your thoughts, use a certain technique, and things should clear up. People really believe that if they just were able to follow this particular path or do this method, everything should work. Then, when that turns out not to be the case, they blame themselves.

That belief is simply extremely naive. We are going through an amazing transformational process. We are delving down through countless layers. We're transforming the ways people have lived and behaved for centuries. We can't simply say a few affirmations or do a simple technique and have it all be done. Growth is a lifelong process.

*

I welcome
a lifetime of growth
and discovery.

*

A lifetime commitment

Change doesn't happen overnight. Individual steps on the path of consciousness can be wonderfully easy, and some steps seem miraculous, but the journey contains many, many steps. And the journey as a whole is not easy. There is not going to be a point when we are "done." It's important to acknowledge that we've made a lifetime commitment to healing and consciousness.

*

I commit myself
to a lifelong journey of healing
and consciousness.

*

You have your own timetable

Consciousness is an ever-deepening, ever-expanding process that never ends. Fortunately, it does become easier and more and more rewarding. But sometimes it gets harder before it gets easier. Sometimes we have to go through deep levels of emotional healing before it starts to feel better.

Wherever you are in the process, don't be discouraged. Everyone has a unique timetable. Don't feel that it's taking you too long or that you should have done it quicker. It very much depends on individual life experiences. Some people have had more pain and trauma in their early lives than others and therefore the depth and extent of their healing process may be greater. But the good thing to remember is that whatever depth you've had to go to in your healing process is what you have to offer to others in their healing process.

*

I respect
my own process. I don't need
to rush things.

*

We need other people

Our society has a strong belief system that we should be able to do everything for ourselves. We ought to be totally self-sufficient. Most of us have really bought that and feel guilty for needing other people or needing connection, love, support, and so on. We repress our dependency needs and try valiantly to appear strong and "together." We even hide our needs from ourselves. Yet, it's impossible for most people to live a satisfying, fulfilling life without deep connection and interdependence with other people. Certainly we need the support and reflection from other people on our journey of healing and consciousness.

*

I need
love and support
from others.

*

Co-dependence versus
interdependence

Co-dependence is the unconscious dependency that exists when we don't recognize and accept our need for others. Interdependence is the conscious acknowledgment of our need for one another.

The need for connection and contact between human beings is very important to acknowledge. Not only do we need intimate relationships with our partners, nuclear families, and close friends, but also we need a sense of connectedness to an extended family, tribe, or community. We need to have a feeling of belonging to a larger group. Ultimately, we need to feel that we are part of the whole human family and connected to all beings on earth.

*

How can I
reach out to create
more sense of connection to
my fellow beings?

*

We are the healing generation

Most of us on a conscious path are spending a majority of our lives healing. Unhealthy patterns that have been handed down for centuries are being healed at this time in history. We are committing ourselves to doing this so that our children will not have to do the same. They will be able to do what they are here to do. This is our piece of the evolutionary process, and we should honor ourselves for it.

*

I recognize
and honor my part in healing
for the next generation.

*

Your healing process
helps others

Whether or not you're in one of the healing or helping professions, just going through your own healing process is inspirational and helpful to anyone else who's dealing with the same kinds of issues that you are.

Helping others is an inevitable part of this process; it's not something you have to try to do. One way or another you will automatically pass on to others what you've learned, as a part of completing your own healing process. You'll find that there are people around you with the same issues, or those with similar problems gravitate to you in some way. You may find yourself sharing your experiences, or you may not ever talk about them. It's just that your life experience is present in your energy field. Other people feel it, they benefit from it, and they receive a life change from making contact with you or being around you.

*

By healing myself,
I'm helping others to heal
themselves.

*

Your healing process
helps your family

If you're working on your own inner healing, you will function as an inspirational role model and will relieve the burden of everyone around you, especially your family members. Children, particularly, always pick up, energetically, their parents' problems, issues, or patterns and perpetuate them in their own lives. If the parent heals on the emotional level, he or she will pass that legacy on to the children, who will not have to deal with the same issues in their own lives.

This is true whether or not your children are grown. If you as a parent begin to deal with your own issues and learn to take better care of yourself, love yourself more, and do your own healing, even your grown children who live across the country or around the world will feel it on some level and will benefit from your process.

*

As I heal,
my whole family is
healing.

*

Living truthfully is difficult

We all have a tendency to just follow along with what other people are doing or what we've always done because it seems like the safest or most comfortable alternative. In that process we often fail to speak or live our truth because we're afraid that someone may not like it or it may lead to some risk or discomfort. Today, how could we follow our own sense of truth and integrity in our lives in a deeper way than usual? How can we take a risk today to speak our truth or live our truth more than we usually do?

*

Today I am
following my own sense
of truth.

*

Practice with small steps

Learning to live by your inner guidance often feels like stepping off the edge of a cliff. It's only by practicing with the small things that we can learn to follow our inner guidance with the big things. That means being able to tune in to what's right for you and having the courage to say yes, or being able to say no when something isn't right for you. These steps create trust in yourself.

Once we've practiced enough, we create a powerful connection to our own inner source. And once we have that, *that* is what can carry us along the path.

*

*Every day I am
deepening my relationship with
my inner guidance.*

*

Share your own experiences

Share your healing process with the people who are important to you. Tell them honestly about it. That's the best way for people to learn. Frame it in terms of yourself, for example, "I have had a fascinating insight recently. I've really seen that this pattern of mine has been affecting my life. I'm beginning to do it differently, and I'm feeling some real change." It's going to spark the interest of the people listening. But if you tell them what they *should* do, their first reaction is, "Don't tell me what to do," or "Why? Do you think I have got a problem?" Don't put them on the defensive.

*

*How do I approach
sharing my changes with those
I love?*

*

It's sufficient for you
to change

You don't have to beat your family or your friends over the head with what you're learning. It's sufficient to make real change in your own life. They will feel it whether or not they even comment on it, because we're so energetically linked with the people we love.

Let them know what you are feeling and experiencing. Share with them what you are learning about yourself. Avoid pressuring them to change or grow in the ways you are. Focus on your own growth process. Chances are, you will see some surprising changes in them after a while.

*

I share
my changes with those close to me,
but I keep the focus
on myself.

*

Recognize the innocent child

Everyone at heart is an innocent child who's doing whatever it has learned to do to survive and feel powerful and safe in this world. Once you recognize all your personality mechanisms for what they are —ways of defending and protecting that child— you can appreciate all aspects of yourself. Then you can also recognize the innocent child and the essential spiritual being within you.

And once you've done that, you can't help but see other people with the same regard you have for yourself. Behind their personality defenses you can see the innocent child, and within that child you'll recognize their spiritual being. And your response to the innocent child and the spiritual being is always love.

*

Within me,
and within everyone,
is an innocent child and
a divine being.

*

*It's not more blessed
to give than to receive*

We have some misconceptions about giving and receiving. People literally try to give more than they receive because giving is considered to be good and receiving is considered to be selfish. This ignores the energetic law of the universe that everything has to find balance. If you give and give, and don't receive equally, you will become drained. You'll be running on empty, trying to give when there's nothing left inside.

It's a wonderful blessing to feel the life force flowing through you, giving to others. But that life energy must be replenished by receiving as well. So it's not more blessed to give than to receive. It's blessed to give and receive equally, because that's what brings balance, integration, and harmony into your life.

*

I *am
learning to give and receive
equally.*

*

You are an artist

Think of your life as a painting, and try to create it the way a painter paints. Listen to the life force within you. Trust it and move with it. Risk trying new colors. Then stand back and look at your painting. What does it tell you about yourself? Your painting gives you wonderful feedback about what is going on inside you.

*

I *am*
the artist of
my life.

*

Life is your masterpiece

Here is one way to look at your life: Every day you are creating a masterpiece. As you create you take the feedback from it, so you see how you can change what you create tomorrow. And you have to be willing to delve very deeply and very honestly into yourself in order to do that. You have to take that reflection and see what it is really teaching you about yourself. Where are you really expressing yourself in a way that feels full and right to you? Where are you holding yourself back? Where is there distortion? How can you heal that? Where is there not truth in this creation, and how can you allow that truth to come forth?

*

I am
*learning daily from my own
creation.*

*

We are here to learn to manifest
spirit into physical form

The spirit—or universal intelligence or experience of oneness—has manifested itself on earth in order to experience twoness. The universe wanted to make love to itself. It wanted to have a relationship with itself. So it created a realm where we can experience separation, individuality, and difference and at the same time that sense of oneness that is always there underneath it all. We're here to learn about oneness and duality, merging and separating. We are here to learn to embrace both these principles, to be able to experience ourselves as one with the universe and at the same time as being unique manifestations of that universal source.

*

I am
separate and unique, and I am
one with all.

*

Honor the male and the female
inside yourself

It is time for both the male principle of discovery, conquest, and separateness and the female principle of connection, spirituality, and oneness to come into equality and balance. We can do this by learning to feel and trust the intuitive feminine power we each have and supporting it with our masculine power of action in the physical world. As we practice listening to our intuition and acting on it moment by moment in every aspect of our daily lives, we bring the female and male sides of our nature into integration and alignment. As more and more of us live in this way, we bring the world into balance.

*

By balancing
my own male and female,
I am bringing the world
into balance.

*

We are the caretakers
of the earth

Because we have been out of touch with our own spirit we have been out of touch with our natural environment. We have been in conflict with nature rather than in harmony with her. In fact, we have seen ourselves as the conquerors of the earth. Now we must recognize that we have been entrusted with the stewardship of the planet. We are the caretakers of the earth.

*

I am
committed to taking care
of this planet.

*

Envisioning the Garden

Imagine the earth restoring herself to her natural balance. More beautiful, varied, abundant, and magical than ever, she is truly a wondrous place to live. Imagine that many of the institutions and structures that were no longer in tune with the needs of the planet have been dismantled or transformed. Humankind has developed wisdom and consciousness and has thereby returned to the Garden.

*

Every day
we are moving closer
to the Garden.

*

GLOSSARY

AFFIRMATION   A strong, positive statement that something is *already so*. It is a way of "making firm" that which you are imagining.

ARCHETYPE   A specific, universal energy pattern or subpersonality. We each potentially contain all of the many archetypes in the universe. Some common archetypes are: the child, the mother, the father, the critic, the warrior.

CHANNEL   To be in touch with and bring through the wisdom and creativity of your own deepest source. (In this book, *channeling* does not refer to the psychic process of trance channeling.)

CONSCIOUSNESS   The awareness and ability to integrate all aspects of ourselves; as human beings, we are involved in an ongoing, ever deepening, lifetime process of becoming conscious.

DISOWN   To reject and deny that a specific energy is a part of oneself. This goes hand in hand with projection. Once we decide that an energy is not part of ourselves, we can only see it in someone else.

FEMININE   The inner intuitive energy of both men and women; the receptive, feeling, being part of ourselves.

HIGHER POWER   A higher intelligence, a fundamental creative power, or energy in the universe which is the source and substance of all that exists. We are used to thinking of this power as being outside ourselves, however it is truly within us. Some other terms to express this are Higher Self, Inner Truth, Inner Source, Universal Source, Universe.

HIGHER SELF   See Higher Power.

INNER SOURCE, UNIVERSAL SOURCE   See Higher Power.

INTEGRATION   Wholeness; specifically, the experience of accepting and expressing all the many aspects of ourselves.

LIFE FORCE   The energy of the universe that flows through all matter.

MASCULINE   The active energy of both men and women; the strong, outer-directed, focused, doing part of ourselves.

MIRRORING   A way of using our outer world as a reflection of our internal process. Since we each create our own reality, our external lives act as a mirror which clearly reflects what is happening inside of us.

POLARITIES   Opposite ends of the same energy spectrum. The nature of the physical plane is duality. Truth comes in pairs of opposites. For every truth, there is an equal and opposite truth. (For a list of some basic polarities, see February 15.)

PROCESS   A continuing, ever changing journey; "going through your process" means learning the lessons you came here to learn.

PROJECTION   The process by which we reject an energy—a feeling or subpersonality—within ourselves, and put it onto others outside ourselves. In so doing, we give it more power than it would otherwise have.

SELVES   Different and distinct energies or subpersonalities that we all have within us. Most people have a certain group that is in charge most of the time ("primary selves"), and an opposite set is repressed ("disowned selves"). Often the repressed selves are struggling to come out, while the dominant selves are frantically trying to stay in control. Some of our many selves may include: the inner child, the protector/controller, the inner critic, the pleaser, the perfectionist, the pusher.

SHADOW   The parts of ourselves (feelings or energies) that we have rejected, repressed, or disowned. When they are not allowed their natural expression, they go underground and "leak out" in distorted ways. We usually project these qualities onto someone else, whom we either judge and dislike, or worship and adore.

UNIVERSE   See Higher Power.

VISUALIZATION   A process of relaxing very deeply and then picturing a desired goal in your mind, which will then be created in the external world.

I N D E X

ABOUT THE AUTHOR

SHAKTI GAWAIN'S first book, *Creative Visualization*, has sold nearly two million copies, with foreign editions in twelve languages, and is now considered by many people to be one of the best self-improvement books ever written. Her subsequent books, *Living in the Light*, *Reflections in the Light*, and *Return to the Garden*, have been equally well-received.

Shakti makes her home in Kauai, Hawaii, where she gives retreats with her husband, Jim Burns, and lectures throughout the United States and Europe.